MAJOR WORLD LEADERS

YASIR ARAFAT

MENACHEM BEGIN

TONY BLAIR

GEORGE W. BUSH

JIMMY CARTER

VICENTE FOX

SADDAM HUSSEIN

HOSNI MUBARAK

VLADIMIR PUTIN

MOHAMMED REZA PAHLAVI

ANWAR SADAT

THE SAUDI ROYAL FAMILY

Yasir Arafat

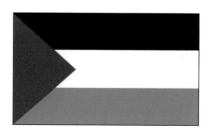

Colleen Madonna Flood Williams

CHELSEA HOUSE
PUBLISHERS
A Haights Cross Communications Company

Philadelphia

CHELSEA HOUSE PUBLISHERS

EDITOR IN CHIEF Sally Cheney
DIRECTOR OF PRODUCTION Kim Shinners
CREATIVE MANAGER Takeshi Takahashi
MANUFACTURING MANAGER Diann Grasse

Staff for YASIR ARAFAT

ASSOCIATE EDITOR Patrick Stone
PRODUCTION ASSISTANT Jaimie Winkler
PICTURE RESEARCH 21st Century Publishing and Communications, Inc.
SERIES AND COVER DESIGNER Takeshi Takahashi
LAYOUT 21st Century Publishing and Communications, Inc.

A Haights Cross Communications ◥ Company

http://www.chelseahouse.com

First Printing

1 3 5 7 9 8 6 4 2

Library of Congress Cataloging-in-Publication Data

Williams, Colleen Madonna Flood.
  Yasir Arafat / Colleen Madonna Flood Williams.
    p. cm.—(Major world leaders)
Summary: A biography of the president of the Palestinian National Authority and winner
of the Nobel Prize.
Includes bibliographical references and index.
  ISBN 0-7910-6941-9 — ISBN 0-7910-7186-3 (pbk.)
  1. Arafat, Yasir, 1929– —Juvenile literature. 2. Palestinian National Authority—Biography—
Juvenile literature. 3. Munaòzòzamat al-Taòhrâir al-Filasòtåinâiyah—Presidents—
Biography—Juvenile literature. [1. Palestinian Arabs—Biography. 2. Arafat, Yasir, 1929–
3. Palestinian Arabs—Biography. 4. Nobel Prizes—Biography.] I. Title. II. Series.
DS126.6.A67 W55 2002
956.9405'092—dc21
                                                                   2002007352

*Dedicated with love to Patrick E. Flood, United States Marine Corps; "Floyd" Flood,
Master Diver, Navy UDT; and Michael Flood, United States Army. As always with love
to Paul Williams and Dillon Meehan, and to Kathleen Flood, who taught me to write.*

TABLE OF CONTENTS

Foreword: On Leadership
Arthur M. Schlesinger, jr.   6

1 Yom al-Nakba, the Day of Catastrophe:
   May 15, 2001   13

2 The Birth of a Symbol: 1929   21

3 Al-Fatah Member: 1949–1963   33

4 From al-Fatah Member to PLO Leader:
   1963–1969   41

5 Black September: 1969–1974   51

6 At Last a Voice: November 13, 1974   65

7 Lebanon, the Intifada, and the
   Nobel Peace Prize   83

8 A Cell Phone and a Submachine Gun:
   March–April 2002   93

   Chronology   102

   Further Reading   104

   Index   106

On Leadership

Arthur M. Schlesinger, jr.

Leadership, it may be said, is really what makes the world go round. Love no doubt smoothes the passage; but love is a private transaction between consenting adults. Leadership is a public transaction with history. The idea of leadership affirms the capacity of individuals to move, inspire, and mobilize masses of people so that they act together in pursuit of an end. Sometimes leadership serves good purposes, sometimes bad; but whether the end is benign or evil, great leaders are those men and women who leave their personal stamp on history.

Now, the very concept of leadership implies the proposition that individuals can make a difference. This proposition has never been universally accepted. From classical times to the present day, eminent thinkers have regarded individuals as no more than the agents and pawns of larger forces, whether the gods and goddesses of the ancient world or, in the modern era, race, class, nation, the dialectic, the will of the people, the spirit of the times, history itself. Against such forces, the individual dwindles into insignificance.

So contends the thesis of historical determinism. Tolstoy's great novel *War and Peace* offers a famous statement of the case. Why, Tolstoy asked, did millions of men in the Napoleonic Wars, denying their human feelings and their common sense, move back and forth across Europe slaughtering their fellows? "The war," Tolstoy answered, "was bound to happen simply because it was bound to happen." All prior history determined it. As for leaders, they, Tolstoy said, "are but the labels that serve to give a name to an end and, like labels, they have the least possible connection with the event." The greater the leader, "the more conspicuous the inevitability and the predestination of every act he commits." The leader, said Tolstoy, is "the slave of history."

Determinism takes many forms. Marxism is the determinism of class. Nazism the determinism of race. But the idea of men and women as the slaves of history runs athwart the deepest human instincts. Rigid determinism abolishes the idea of human freedom—the assumption of free choice that underlies every move we make, every word we speak, every thought we think. It abolishes the idea of human responsibility, since it is manifestly unfair to reward or punish people for actions that are by definition beyond their control. No one can live consistently by any deterministic creed. The Marxist states prove this themselves by their extreme susceptibility to the cult of leadership.

More than that, history refutes the idea that individuals make no difference. In December 1931 a British politician crossing Fifth Avenue in New York City between 76th and 77th Streets around 10:30 P.M. looked in the wrong direction and was knocked down by an automobile—a moment, he later recalled, of a man aghast, a world aglare: "I do not understand why I was not broken like an eggshell or squashed like a gooseberry." Fourteen months later an American politician, sitting in an open car in Miami, Florida, was fired on by an assassin; the man beside him was hit. Those who believe that individuals make no difference to history might well ponder whether the next two decades would have been the same had Mario Constasino's car killed Winston Churchill in 1931 and Giuseppe Zangara's bullet killed Franklin Roosevelt in 1933. Suppose, in addition, that Lenin had died of typhus in Siberia in 1895 and that Hitler had been killed on the western front in 1916. What would the 20th century have looked like now?

For better or for worse, individuals do make a difference. "The notion that a people can run itself and its affairs anonymously," wrote the philosopher William James, "is now well known to be the silliest of absurdities. Mankind does nothing save through initiatives on the part of inventors, great or small, and imitation by the rest of us—these are the sole factors in human progress. Individuals of genius show the way, and set the patterns, which common people then adopt and follow."

Leadership, James suggests, means leadership in thought as well as in action. In the long run, leaders in thought may well make the greater difference to the world. "The ideas of economists and political philosophers, both when they are right and when they are wrong," wrote John Maynard Keynes, "are more powerful than is commonly understood. Indeed the world is ruled by little else. Practical men, who believe themselves to be quite exempt from any intellectual influences, are usually the slaves of some defunct economist. . . . The power of vested interests is vastly exaggerated compared with the gradual encroachment of ideas."

But, as Woodrow Wilson once said, "Those only are leaders of men, in the general eye, who lead in action. . . . It is at their hands that new thought gets its translation into the crude language of deeds." Leaders in thought often invent in solitude and obscurity, leaving to later generations the tasks of imitation. Leaders in action—the leaders portrayed in this series—have to be effective in their own time.

And they cannot be effective by themselves. They must act in response to the rhythms of their age. Their genius must be adapted, in a phrase from William James, "to the receptivities of the moment." Leaders are useless without followers. "There goes the mob," said the French politician, hearing a clamor in the streets. "I am their leader. I must follow them." Great leaders turn the inchoate emotions of the mob to purposes of their own. They seize on the opportunities of their time, the hopes, fears, frustrations, crises, potentialities. They succeed when events have prepared the way for them, when the community is awaiting to be aroused, when they can provide the clarifying and organizing ideas. Leadership completes the circuit between the individual and the mass and thereby alters history.

It may alter history for better or for worse. Leaders have been responsible for the most extravagant follies and most monstrous crimes that have beset suffering humanity. They have also been vital in such gains as humanity has made in individual freedom, religious and racial tolerance, social justice, and respect for human rights.

There is no sure way to tell in advance who is going to lead for good and who for evil. But a glance at the gallery of men and women in Major World Leaders suggests some useful tests.

One test is this: Do leaders lead by force or by persuasion? By command or by consent? Through most of history leadership was exercised by the divine right of authority. The duty of followers was to defer and to obey. "Theirs not to reason why/Theirs but to do and die." On occasion, as with the so-called enlightened despots of the 18th century in Europe, absolutist leadership was animated by humane purposes. More often, absolutism nourished the passion for domination, land, gold, and conquest and resulted in tyranny.

The great revolution of modern times has been the revolution of equality. "Perhaps no form of government," wrote the British historian James Bryce in his study of the United States, *The American Commonwealth*, "needs great leaders so much as democracy." The idea that all people should be equal in their legal condition has undermined the old structure of authority, hierarchy, and deference. The revolution of equality has had two contrary effects on the nature of leadership. For equality, as Alexis de Tocqueville pointed out in his great study *Democracy in America*, might mean equality in servitude as well as equality in freedom.

"I know of only two methods of establishing equality in the political world," Tocqueville wrote. "Rights must be given to every citizen, or none at all to anyone . . . save one, who is the master of all." There was no middle ground "between the sovereignty of all and the absolute power of one man." In his astonishing prediction of 20th-century totalitarian dictatorship, Tocqueville explained how the revolution of equality could lead to the *Führerprinzip* and more terrible absolutism than the world had ever known.

But when rights are given to every citizen and the sovereignty of all is established, the problem of leadership takes a new form, becomes more exacting than ever before. It is easy to issue commands and enforce them by the rope and the stake, the concentration camp and the *gulag*. It is much harder to use argument and achievement to overcome opposition and win consent. The Founding Fathers of the United States understood the difficulty. They believed that history had given them the opportunity to decide, as Alexander Hamilton wrote in the first Federalist Paper, whether men are indeed capable of basing government on "reflection and choice, or whether they are forever destined to depend . . . on accident and force."

Government by reflection and choice called for a new style of leadership and a new quality of followership. It required leaders to be responsive to popular concerns, and it required followers to be active and informed participants in the process. Democracy does not eliminate emotion from politics; sometimes it fosters demagoguery; but it is confident that, as the greatest of democratic leaders put it, you cannot fool all of the people all of the time. It measures leadership by results and retires those who overreach or falter or fail.

It is true that in the long run despots are measured by results too. But they can postpone the day of judgment, sometimes indefinitely, and in the meantime they can do infinite harm. It is also true that democracy is no guarantee of virtue and intelligence in government, for the voice of the people is not necessarily the voice of God. But democracy, by assuring the right of opposition, offers built-in resistance to the evils inherent in absolutism. As the theologian Reinhold Niebuhr summed it up, "Man's capacity for justice makes democracy possible, but man's inclination to justice makes democracy necessary."

A second test for leadership is the end for which power is sought. When leaders have as their goal the supremacy of a master race or the promotion of totalitarian revolution or the acquisition and exploitation of colonies or the protection of greed and privilege or the preservation of personal power, it is likely that their leadership will do little to advance the cause of humanity. When their goal is the abolition of slavery, the liberation of women, the enlargement of opportunity for the poor and powerless, the extension of equal rights to racial minorities, the defense of the freedoms of expression and opposition, it is likely that their leadership will increase the sum of human liberty and welfare.

Leaders have done great harm to the world. They have also conferred great benefits. You will find both sorts in this series. Even "good" leaders must be regarded with a certain wariness. Leaders are not demigods; they put on their trousers one leg after another just like ordinary mortals. No leader is infallible, and every leader needs to be reminded of this at regular intervals. Irreverence irritates leaders but is their salvation. Unquestioning submission corrupts leaders and demeans followers. Making a cult of a leader is always a mistake. Fortunately hero worship generates its own antidote. "Every hero," said Emerson, "becomes a bore at last."

The signal benefit the great leaders confer is to embolden the rest of us to live according to our own best selves, to be active, insistent, and resolute in affirming our own sense of things. For great leaders attest to the reality of human freedom against the supposed inevitabilities of history. And they attest to the wisdom and power that may lie within the most unlikely of us, which is why Abraham Lincoln remains the supreme example of great leadership. A great leader, said Emerson, exhibits new possibilities to all humanity. "We feed on genius . . . . Great men exist that there may be greater men."

Great leaders, in short, justify themselves by emancipating and empowering their followers. So humanity struggles to master its destiny, remembering with Alexis de Tocqueville: "It is true that around every man a fatal circle is traced beyond which he cannot pass; but within the wide verge of that circle he is powerful and free; as it is with man, so with communities." ◾

LEBANON

GOLAN HEIGHTS
territory claimed
by SYRIA and occupied
by ISRAEL

Qiryat
Shemona

SYRIA

GOLAN HEIGHTS

Haifa

Lake
Tiberias

Afiq
En Gev

Nazareth

MEDITERRANEAN
SEA

Janin

Netanya

Tulkarm

Nablus

Jordan River

Tel Aviv-Yafo

WEST

WEST BANK AND
GAZA STRIP
territories
under provisional status
since 1993

Ramle

Ramallah

Gilgal

AMMAN

JERUSALEM

Jericho

Ashdod

Bethlehem

BANK

GAZA STRIP

Gaza

Hebron

Dead Sea

Beersheba

ISRAEL

JORDAN

EGYPT

Elat

SAUDI
ARABIA

Gulf of Aqaba

The creation of Israel is a bitter memory for most Palestinians, hundreds of thousands of whom were driven from their homes in 1948. The anniversary of Israel's nationhood is remembered by Palestinians as Yom al-Nakba, the Day of Catastrophe, and marked by protests. Here, Palestinians demonstrate in Gaza City on May 15, 2001.

1

Yom al-Nakba, the Day of Catastrophe: May 15, 2001

May 15, 1948, is the birthday of the official state of Israel. Seen through the eyes of a Palestinian such as Yasir Arafat, it is also the commemoration of the death of Palestinian freedom. To the Palestinians, May 15 is a sort of national holiday akin to a day of mourning. While the Israelis might be celebrating the birth of their nation, the Palestinians are denigrating it. In Palestine, May 15 is referred to as Yom al-Nakba, Arabic for "the Day of Catastrophe."

On May 15, 2001, tens of thousands of Arafat's people took to the streets. The Palestinian people were demonstrating angrily against the anniversary of the establishment of the nation of Israel. Throughout the Israeli-occupied Palestinian territories, Palestinians and Israeli Defense Forces battled in the streets. Fifty-three years had passed since the creation of the state of Israel, and the anger and violence between the Israelis and Palestinians had only grown.

Just prior to the three minutes of silence observed by Palestinians at noon, news spread throughout Palestine of a conflict between the Israelis and a group of Palestinians near a checkpoint between Gaza and Israel. The Israelis reported that the Palestinians had punctuated their demonstration with a mortar bomb. In response, the Israelis had returned fire, and an Israeli tank shell had claimed the life of one of the bodyguards of Ahmad Yassin, the spiritual leader of the Islamic militant group Hamas. It had also injured six other Palestinians.

Palestinian authorities watched as the mood of their people worsened. The people were asked to peacefully engage in a march to demonstrate their feelings. During the march, more violence broke out between the Israeli soldiers and the Palestinian demonstrators.

In the midst of all this madness, Arafat publicly addressed the Palestinian people via a recorded speech. His speech was broadcast on television stations and over public address systems throughout Palestine. As Palestinians marched, demonstrated, and fought skirmishes against the Israeli soldiers, Arafat was right there with his people, through the magic of communications media.

His words were typically supportive of the people of Palestine and defiant towards the Israelis. His timing was well suited to the circumstances, too. When all seemed darkest to his people, his image and voice were everywhere, urging them to remember their cause.

Wearing his signature uniform, a black-and-white *keffiyeh* topping off olive-green military attire, Arafat, who was ever mindful of his image as the "symbol of Palestine," gave the Palestinian nation a pep talk and gave the Israelis a tongue-lashing. He reached out to the common Palestinians, praising

Arafat wanted his words to be heard by as many of his people as possible, and television proved to be his ally. Here, Palestinians watch the speech as their leader delivers it—from a tire shop at a refugee camp in Bethlehem.

each for their resilience in their struggles with these words: "Our steadfast Palestinian masses, people of exceeding strength. On this day, we commemorate the catastrophe that befell our people on May 15, 1948—our entire people. Our people have experienced fifty-three years of tribulation, pain, and dispersal in and outside the homeland."

He threatened the Israelis by iterating that his people would not quit before reaching their goals: "With their deep-rooted faith, our people remain committed to their principles in the face of the grand conspiracy with an unrelenting willpower," he stated with conviction. "They will not bow their heads or give in."

His self-righteous anger was probably never more evident than when he denounced Israel: "The attempt to falsify history by missiles, shells, and tanks will not succeed. This is so because we have right on our side and we defend a just cause that cannot be wiped out by tank shells, poisonous gases, internationally prohibited weapons, or guided missiles."

Arafat continued to incite outrage among the Palestinian crowds demonstrating in the streets as he took issue with the entire world. "The hour of the awakening of the world conscience from its deep slumber has come," he said. "The hour of international legitimacy has come to tell the aggressors: Enough military escalation and enough killing and destruction of the Palestinian people, who will not be defeated. Until when will the world continue to turn a deaf ear to Palestinian blood-shed at the hands of the Israeli occupiers and settlers? Are the Palestinian people not entitled to live free in their homeland, just like all other peoples in the world?"

The Palestinian president's tone was both accusatory and resentful as he uttered: "International legitimacy, which the world had called upon us to recognize and to abide by its resolutions, is being trampled every day in Palestine by the Israeli occupation army and its military escalation and the siege imposed on our cities, villages, and refugee camps."

Arafat also used his public address that day to once more clarify his demands upon the state of Israel. His vision of the road to the end of violence between Palestinians and Israelis was illustrated with the following pointed expressions:

> On this day of al-Nakba, I reiterate that the path to peace is crystal clear, represented by the full and compre-hensive withdrawal of the Israeli occupation army and settlers from all Palestinian and Arab territories up to the lines of June 4, 1967. It is also represented by the resolution of the refugee issue based on Resolution 194 and all resolutions of international legitimacy.

In this speech, Arafat spoke again of the hopes, dreams, and spirits of the Palestinians marching in the streets. Drawing

April 11, 2002: These two Palestinian women walk amid the rubble of homes destroyed by Israeli defense forces in the Jenin refugee camp, the scene of some of the worst fighting of the Israeli-Palestinian conflict. The camp's 24-hour curfew has been lifted for three hours so that the home-bound residents might find new supplies of food and water to tide them over until the next opportunity.

himself up, as if to illustrate that he did, indeed, measure up to the larger-than-life image his name conjured up in the minds of many throughout the world, the self-proclaimed freedom fighter, now visibly aging, cajoled his compatriots: "The blind military force the Israeli occupation government is launching against our people in order to destroy them and wipe out their existence will never achieve peace and security and will not enforce capitulation on our people. The flare will continue to burn and light up the difficult path before Palestinian

Five-year-old Ala Mitwali, right, looks from the window of her home in the Al-Amri refugee camp, south of the West Bank town of Ramallah in July of 2000. With her are her three-year-old brother, Mohammed, and her grandmother, Subha. Subha Mitwali, 74, has been a refugee for over 50 years but still hopes to return one day to her home, in what is now southern Tel Aviv.

generations, one generation after another, until the flag of Palestine is raised over holy Jerusalem."

Steadfast, he continued, "There can be no peace or stability while the Palestinian refugees are displaced outside their homeland, because their right is a sacred and legitimate one. It is the responsibility of the entire international community to ensure and guarantee this right to the Palestinian refugees."

Still, Arafat knew he must also show to the world a willingness to work toward peace. To this end, he remarked, "Let the

Egyptian-Jordanian initiative, alongside the agreements, the Mitchell Committee's report, and the resolutions of international legitimacy, especially Resolutions 242 and 338, be the basis of our efforts [to put] a just, comprehensive, and lasting peace process back on track. This is for the sake of the Palestinian people, the Israeli people, and for the sake of the people of the Middle East region. It is the time for justice and international legitimacy to champion right in Palestine, as they have championed it in other areas of the world."

By the end of the day, at least four Palestinians would be dead and over two hundred injured. Arafat and the Palestinian nation had once more endured a day of catastrophe. There were many such days in their past, and many more to come in their future; but somehow it seemed the resilient Arafat and his Palestinian people would survive them all.

The city of Jerusalem is a holy place for Jews, Muslims, and Christians, and it has been an ongoing point of contention between the Palestinians and Israelis for decades. Yasir Arafat has long claimed, too, that Jerusalem is the place of his birth. However, some experts believe he was actually born in Cairo, Egypt, and that Arafat calls Jerusalem his place of birth for political reasons.

2

The Birth
of a Symbol:
1929

Yasir Arafat was born Mohammed Abdel Rahman Abdel
Raouf Arafat al-Qudua al-Husseini. By Western standards,
this is quite a large name for a little child, but by Palestinian
standards there was nothing abnormal about his name.

To better understand it, Arafat's birth name can be broken
down into five segments. The first segment, Mohammed Abdel
Rahman, is his first name. The second segment, Abdel Raouf, was
his father's name. His grandfather's name was Arafat, which is the
next segment. His family's name is al-Qudua, the fourth segment. The
fifth segment indicates that his family is part of the al-Husseini clan.

Arafat was born about 11 years after the fall of the Ottoman
Empire. After the Empire's defeat in 1918, Great Britain was given
control of Palestine, which had become a territory administered
by the League of Nations. These events prior to Arafat's birth

would help to set the stage for the all of the later events of his life.

There has been some argument over the date of Arafat's birth: August 4 or 24, 1929. The place of his birth, too, has been a point of contention for many years. Arafat has said that he was born in Jerusalem, Palestine, but his birth certificate says that he was born in Cairo, Egypt.

For many years, there were two main explanations generally given for this disagreement by loyal Arafat followers. One was that his birth certificate was forged to allow him easier access to the educational system in Egypt. Another has to do with the circumstances of his birth. Arafat's mother had traveled alone from Cairo to Jerusalem to give birth to Arafat, and this was considered improper for a Muslim wife because she left her husband to have her child in her family's home. To protect his mother's good name, as well as that of his family, Arafat's birth certificate was forged to make it look as though he had been born in Egypt.

Others say that Arafat's early years in Cairo were so unhappy that he decided not to acknowledge them, preferring to remember the happier years he spent in Jerusalem in the house of his uncle. And yet another explanation is that Arafat, as a master propagandist, felt it was better for him as a leader of the Palestinian people to be seen as a native of Jerusalem.

Despite the varying stories told about Arafat's birth, most experts have come to agree that he was born in Cairo, Egypt. Yet, if you were to look on Arafat's website today, his birth place is still listed as Jerusalem, Palestine.

To understand Arafat's steadfast insistence that he was born in Jerusalem, one must understand the tragedy of his early years and his intense desire to succeed. His childhood was not a happy one. He was not a handsome child, nor the best of students. Worse still, after losing his mother at an early age, he never became close to his father. Perhaps, too, he blamed his father for moving his family from Jerusalem to Cairo.

Arafat's father, Abdel Raouf Arafat al-Qudua al-Husseini, was born in Gaza. His mother, Zahwa Abu Saud, was from Jerusalem. His father moved his family from Palestine to Egypt, hoping to become a wealthy landowner. He believed that a great amount of valuable land in the Abbasiya District of Cairo had belonged to his mother, and he was certain that after her death this land should have become his. Unfortunately, the land had not been in his mother's family for over a century. Abdel Raouf would, nevertheless, go to his grave claiming that he had been cheated out of his birthright, even though the courts in the region disagreed with him.

Arafat's father had established their family home in al-Sakakini, a neighborhood in Cairo, Egypt, at the time of his son's birth. Arafat was the sixth of seven children. His mother died of a kidney ailment when Arafat was only four or five years old. His father quickly remarried, but his second marriage was unsuccessful. Arafat and his younger brother, Fathi, were then sent to live with an uncle on his mother's side of the family, who lived in the old city of Jerusalem. Uncle Selim Abul Saoud's house was near the Wailing Wall, the Dome of the Rock, and the Mosque of Omar.

It has been said that Arafat and Fathi were happy here. Uncle Selim did not beat the boys, as their father had done. Instead, Arafat and Fathi were loved and made to feel as if they were truly members of their new family. The young Arafat came to love the sights, sounds, and smells of Jerusalem, the city of his forefathers. But he did not remain in his uncle's care for long. In 1937 Abdel Raouf sent for his two sons because their older sister Inam was now old enough to care for them.

Arafat started attending school in Cairo. Although Inam

Yasir Arafat and his brother, Fathi, attend the funeral of their sister Inam Arafat. Arafat and his sister were very close, and it was she who actually spent many years raising Arafat and his younger brother when they were boys.

truly tried to provide a loving and stable household for her younger brothers, their father was a different matter. He was a good provider, but Abdel Raouf was far from a loving parent, and Arafat's home life again turned unhappy.

Abdel Raouf remarried several times, but never successfully, so the children had a succession of stepmothers who challenged Inam's position as their surrogate mother. Meanwhile, their father was obsessed with obtaining what he considered to be his birthright: the land that had once belonged to his mother's family.

The Palestinian leader was therefore born and raised in Egypt under the strict hand of his father. Later, when his father died, Arafat refused to return to Egypt for his father's funeral, and he has never publicly visited his father's grave. Perhaps he never forgave his father for moving to Egypt, or perhaps he could not forgive his father for beating him or for taking him away from his beloved Uncle Selim. Only Arafat can clarify this, but he will not speak about his childhood or his father.

Most of Arafat's biographers agree that Inam tried to protect her brothers from the heavy hand of her father. This proved impossible, however. Arafat began to run away to the house of his Cairo relatives, the Awad al-Akhbar family, to avoid punishments. Here, between the ages of 9 and 15, he began to learn more about the Koran and his Islamic background.

During his school years in Cairo, the young Mohammed Abdel Rahman was given the nickname "Yasir." Some accounts say that his family gave him this nickname; others say that he was given this name by early schoolmates; still other accounts say that he did not become Yasir until his college years. All accounts, however, agree that Yasir means "easygoing."

Yasir, as he is now more universally known, was not an overachiever when it came to his studies, but he *was* an overachiever when it came to life in the streets. The young Arafat proved to be a leader early in life, forming and controlling a group of neighborhood children as if he was a troop commander. He was a soldier at heart from a very early age.

Around 1946, Arafat stepped up from leading street gangs to become a member of the more trusted associates of Hajj Amin al-Husseini, the Mufti of Palestine. The Mufti had come to reside in a suburb just outside of Cairo, Egypt. With him, by chance, came one of Arafat's maternal uncles, Sheikh Hassan Abul Saoud.

Sheikh Hassan Abul Saoud soon adopted Arafat and his family. Arafat saw his chance to rise above the common merchant status of his father by attaching himself to his uncle the Sheikh, for through the Sheikh, Yasir could gain political knowledge and power. He could also gain access to the inner circles of the Mufti.

The Mufti was the acknowledged leader of the Arabs of Palestine. In the past, the Mufti had been associated with Nazi Germany and with Adolf Hitler himself. After being persecuted for his connections to the Nazi leaders of World War II, the Mufti had sought asylum in Egypt.

In 1947, eighteen years after his birth, Arafat graduated from high school in Cairo, and in November of that year a war broke out in the Middle East. The General Assembly of the United Nations had made the resolution to partition Palestine between the Arab and Jewish communities. The Arab community disagreed with this resolution, and the war between the Israelis and Arabs began.

By that time, Arafat had begun studying engineering at King Fuad I University, which was later to become Cairo University. Again, Arafat proved that scholarly studies were not his strong suit, and his grades were unimpressive. But the university gave him his first taste of university-level politics. Arafat was much more interested in attaching himself to young students from powerful Palestinian families than he was in his studies. He frequented student gatherings and Palestinian meetings. Poorer Palestinian students who associated with Arafat began receiving scholarships from Sheikh Hassan with Arafat's help, and this expanded his group of followers.

Hajj Amin al-Husseini, the Mufti of Palestine, was the acknowledged leader of the Palestinians during Arafat's youth. It was the Mufti who helped the young Arafat get his first taste of political involvement in Palestinian affairs.

To strengthen his connections, Arafat served as a messenger for the Mufti and his Higher Arab Committee. He delivered letters and messages to the surrounding Arab countries and to members of the Arab League, collected donations for the Arab cause, and became the Mufti's eyes and ears on Egyptian campuses.

Meanwhile, the Mufti's Arab supporters, the Holy Strugglers in Palestine, began receiving the remnants of World War II armaments from the Bedouins of today's Libya. These arms—rifles, light machine guns, and sub-machine guns—were acquired by Sheikh Hassan Abul Saoud and his men, who were working in the service of the Mufti. Through his contact with his relative the Sheikh, and the Sheikh's acquaintances, Arafat had his first real taste of the life of a soldier during these years. By the end of 1947, he had become involved in the buying and shipping of arms.

By the winter of 1948, the fighting had started over the partitioning of Palestine. The Jewish military experienced its first true victory in the spring, and Arabs were cast out of their homes, becoming exiled refugees. Troops from throughout the Arab world were organized and sent to fight in defense of Palestine. Syrians and Egyptians moved to support their Palestinian brothers and sisters, but Arafat was not among them. He remained in school.

On April 7, 1948, Abdel Kader al-Husseini, an important leader of anti-British and anti-Jewish riots, was killed; the news shocked Arafat and millions of other supporters of the Palestinian cause. On April 9, a massacre took place at Deir Yassin. More than 100 men, women, and children were killed by the forces of the Irgun, led by Menachem Begin, and the Stern Gang, Jewish radicals known for terrorism. Again, the Palestinians and Arabs were stunned. It was unbelievable that the Palestinian forces were facing defeat.

Palestinian students at the University of Cairo gathered together. Arafat was among these students. They burned their

Arab refugees flee Galilee during the Arab-Israeli war in 1948.

books, writing tablets, student identification cards, and class schedules. They declared their loyalty to the Palestinian cause and their determination to join the war.

The leader of this demonstration, Hamid Abu Sitta, had been trained to fight in one of Abdel Kader's camps. He was older than Arafat, but familiar with him. At first, he was reluctant to allow Arafat to join in the fighting, but Arafat convinced the reluctant Hamid Abu Sitta to take him along on the journey to Gaza.

Israeli Cabinet Ministers celebrate the creation of Israel on May 14, 1948, by singing their new national anthem, "Hatikvah," at the Tel Aviv Art Museum.

Arafat fought in the Muslim Brothers' volunteer units against the Israelis at Kibbutz Kfar Darom. The attack was unsuccessful, and a week later Egyptian military forces overtook the Muslim Brothers' volunteer troops. Although both units were fighting for the same cause, the Egyptian troops disarmed the Muslim Brothers' soldiers. Apparently, they did not want help from irregular troops.

Angered, but not completely discouraged, Arafat traveled to Jerusalem to take part in the fighting once again. The period of British administration of the area—the British mandate—was over, and David Ben-Gurion announced the birth of the nation of Israel. Palestinians now had more to fight for, and to fight against, than ever.

In Jerusalem the local Palestinian army was disarmed by

the soldiers of the Transjordanian Arab Legion, a military group under British command. Arab leaders that Arafat had come to admire and respect had let the Palestinians down. Once more, Arafat was forced off the battlefield.

It seems that Arafat was born to be a refugee. During his early years, he was an emotional refugee, a young boy without a mother. As he grew, he ended up becoming a military refugee, a soldier without arms or a battlefield. Once he matured, he realized his potential as the symbolic leader of the Palestinian political refugees.

Certainly, Arafat was born to become the symbol of Palestine's struggles. Today, he is referred to by Palestinians like Jibril Rajoub, head of the Preventive Security Service in the West Bank, as the symbol of national freedom. There may be many mysteries that surround Arafat, but it is no mystery that on August 4 (or 24), 1929, the child was born who would grow into the man identified with the Palestinian struggle.

Some call Arafat a terrorist; others call him a hero. The label given to Arafat depends upon who is speaking. Almost all would agree, however, that Yasir Arafat has indeed become the recognized world leader of the Palestinian people.

A view of the city skyline of Cairo, Egypt, Yasir Arafat's place of birth.

3

Al-Fatah Member: 1949–1963

I n 1949, Israel had won the war. The State of Israel now controlled two-thirds of Palestine. Of the 1.3 million Palestine Arabs, half were now refugees. Jordan took control of what is now referred to as the West Bank. This area includes the western hills of Judea and Samaria. Egyptian military rule took over the Gaza Strip, a thin length of land on the southern coast of Palestine.

Yasir Arafat was returning to school. He considered finishing his engineering degree in the United States or Canada. Instead, he returned to Cairo.

Back at the university, Arafat almost immediately joined a group of students who called themselves the Egyptian Union of Students. Their major goals were to resolve the causes of the 1948 loss and to punish King Farouk for his part in it. No Palestinian students were allowed to join their group. This was an Egyptian association, but

Arafat qualified as Egyptian because of his Cairo birth.

True to his dual nature, Arafat also joined a group of students called the Palestinian Students' Association or the Federation of Palestinian Students. He was Egyptian when he wanted to be and Palestinian when he wanted to be. Soon, however, he would be Palestinian and nothing else in his eyes and in the eyes of the world.

In 1949 Arafat also began publishing a magazine entitled *The Voice of Palestine*. The magazine had no ties to any recognized ideological group, but it did cry out for a movement based on freeing the Palestinians and defeating the imperialists. As was Arafat's policy, the magazine tried not to alienate anyone who might be of use to the Palestinian cause in the future.

Next, the 22-year-old Arafat was elected chairman of the Federation of Palestinian Students. Barely two years after this achievement, the 5'4" Arafat took the reins of the General Union of Palestinian Students. This group was much older and larger than the Federation of Palestinian Students and had much deeper ties to the Arab nations throughout the Middle East.

The aim of the General Union of Palestinian Students was to serve as a uniting entity for Palestinian students. This was the voice that represented their views to the educational and, more importantly, political powers. It was also a group that sought to prepare the future leaders of the Palestinian nation. Finally, this group was to support the role of Palestinian students in the battle against the occupation of Palestinian territory.

Surprisingly, a year prior to taking over the General Union of Palestinian Students, Arafat had gone to fight in the Suez Canal battles. The Egyptian people had begun demanding that the British leave the Suez Canal. When in 1950 the British refused, groups like the Muslim Brotherhood and the fascist group Young Egypt began waging strikes against the British troops that were stationed in the Canal Zone. Arafat traveled to the Canal Zone with volunteer units from the Muslim Brotherhood with the goal of helping the Egyptians harass the British troops who were stationed there.

In 1952, Egypt's monarchy was overthrown by its own military forces, and General Mohammed Naguib was put in charge of the nation. Everyone knew, however, that Colonel Gamal Abdel Nasser held a great deal of power within this regime. Nasser quickly became known as the recognized, though not the official, leader of Egypt and the ultimate power broker in the Arab world. King Farouk was sent into exile.

The next year, Nasser and his supporters took control of Egypt away from General Naguib. The Muslim Brotherhood was not pleased with this change, however, and they plotted against Nasser secretly. By 1954, Nassar had outlawed the Muslim Brotherhood, and many of its members had been arrested.

In October of 1954, while Nasser was in Alexandria giving a speech, the Muslim Brotherhood tried, unsuccessfully, to assassinate him. Nasser's vengeance was swift. More members and known associates of the Muslim Brotherhood throughout Egypt were arrested. Arafat's first arrest was a result of this response to the assassination attempt. More than two months later, Arafat was released.

Arafat must have decided at this point that it would be better to get along with Nasser than to be his enemy. He could accomplish this within Egypt, but not this close to Nasser's forces along the Suez. Nasser stood proudly for Arab nationalism, however, and anyone who stood for Arab nationalism stood against the Israelis. This also meant Nasser would claim to support the Palestinian cause.

Arafat retreated to the Gaza Strip, which at that time was controlled by Egypt. Palestinian fighters, who were known as *fedayeen*, or "self-sacrificers," were using the Gaza Strip as their access point for raids into Israel. The Egyptian government allowed them to do so. Here, Arafat became known as a daring fighter and a heroic leader.

Unfortunately for Arafat and his followers, Egypt soon decided to put an end to their exploits. Egypt was concerned

Gamal Abdel Nasser, President of Egypt, at first tolerated the Muslim Brotherhood to which Arafat belonged. However, his desire to have good relationships with Western nations turned him against the Brotherhood, and he had its members arrested. Arafat consequently decided to retreat to the Gaza Strip.

about its own political place in the world, not that of the Palestinians, and raids against Israel were not making Egypt any friends among the more powerful Western nations. To fix this problem, Nasser issued orders that those who refused to stop raiding Israel were to be imprisoned. Arafat decided it was time to return to Cairo once again.

Cairo in 1955 could not have been a happy place for Arafat. Many of his friends had been imprisoned. The ruling Egyptian government, headed by Nasser, did not recognize or need him. To add insult to injury, he was called upon by Nasser's government to serve in its military. Arafat was sent to be trained as a bomb disposal officer. After three months, he completed his training and became a first lieutenant.

The years passed. His friends married. He did not.

Arafat found work in Kuwait as an engineer for the Public Works Department. In October of 1959, he and four of his friends gathered together for a special purpose. His friends included Salah Khalaf, otherwise known as Abu Iyad, and Khalil al-Wazir, alias Abu Jihad, who were working as teachers and were Arafat's longtime friends. The other friends were Farouk Kaddoumi, or Abu Lutf, who was working for Kuwait's Health Department, and Khaled al-Hassan, also called Abu Said, who held a government official's position in the Kuwait Ministry of the Interior. Together these five men would form a new political group called al-Fatah.

Fatah is said to be a reverse acronym for Harakat al-Tahrir al-Falistiniya, the Palestinian Liberation Movement. The letters in Fatah form a word that means "conquest" in Arabic. Also, when reversed again, the letters spell "hataf"—the Arabic word for death.

Starting in November of 1959, the group began a publication that called for the creation of an independent Palestinian nation. The publication was called *Filastinuna,* or *Our Palestine.* The publication also used "armed struggle" as one of its most important slogans. Its paramount message was that Palestinians must set up their own government and begin their own military actions against Israel.

Al-Fatah condemned the West for helping to create Israel and for continuing to support Israel's existence. Furthermore, with a push from Arafat, al-Fatah refused to become involved in Arab feuds. It began to suggest the idea of Palestinians pledging loyalty only to other Palestinians in their "armed struggle" to take back Palestine.

In a world where the Palestinian youth saw the Muslim Brotherhood, communists, Arab nationalists, and other groups as having disappointed or, worse yet, deceived Palestinians time after time, al-Fatah's message began to gain support. Slowly but surely, al-Fatah's following grew.

Then the union between Egypt and Syria broke in 1961, dissolving the United Arab Republic. The political environment in the Middle East was ripe for a new entity to catch the hopes and spirits of Palestinians, and al-Fatah began to attract more and more members.

Arafat and his al-Fatah partners used their publication to speak to the fears and frustrations of the Palestinians. One might imagine that politically aware Palestinians of all ages were asking themselves many questions. If the Arabs could not maintain unity among themselves, how could they maintain it with the Palestinians? Would they even bother to try? Could Palestinians depend on them at all? It was time for a new movement among the Palestinians, and al-Fatah was there to provide just that.

Arafat was moving toward his goal of an independent Palestinian state once more. Now he and a close circle of his friends were in the background, pulling the strings of their own movement. Al-Fatah was growing stronger each year.

Arafat was no longer a mere messenger for the Mufti, learning the intricacies of military politics. Al-Fatah was not the General Union of Palestinian Students, the Egyptian Union of Students, or the Palestinian Students' Association, where Yasir had learned about college politics. Arafat was now embarking on a journey that would allow him to apply all that he had learned in the past while learning even more about social politics.

Along with several of his associates, Arafat traveled to Syria late in 1961 to meet with the Syrians, who were opposed to Nasser at the time. Syria had much earlier in the year broken ties with Egypt, and Arafat was well aware that Syria's border with Israel offered a strategic advantage to anyone who wished to fight against the Israelis. He was also well aware that Syria considered Palestine a part of Syria and was very anti-Israeli. Despite Arafat's earlier claims through al-Fatah of a desire to remain removed from all Arab disputes, Arafat and al-Fatah were choosing Syria over Egypt.

In Syria, Arafat and al-Fatah grew stronger. Palestinians willing to join and be trained to serve in al-Fatah's ranks were paid three times the monthly salary of six sterlings that Syrian army troops received, which made for an irresistible offer for many. But Arafat was not just counting on attracting young men with higher pay. He knew that Syria was home to more than 150,000 Palestinian refugees at this time, and al-Fatah's Palestinian agenda attracted many young men from the refugee camps to join the al-Fatah troops.

Al-Fatah's luck continued. Abu Jihad had struck up a friendship years ago in Cairo with an exiled Algerian named Amhad ben Bella. Ben Bella was no longer in exile. In fact, he was now the president of Algeria, and he agreed to allow Arafat to send troops to his country for training.

By 1963, al-Fatah had soldiers training in Algeria, Iraq, and Syria. The training in Iraq did not last long, however. The new regime in Iraq wanted to require Arafat's al-Fatah troops to undergo Iraqi programming. Arafat refused and pulled his men out of Iraq. The only indoctrination al-Fatah soldiers would undergo would be whatever Arafat and al-Fatah decided it should be.

Arafat was now 34 years old. His political skills had been sharpened by his contacts with members of the Syrian, Iraqi, and Algerian governments; he knew what course of action al-Fatah must follow.

Al-Fatah and its army were growing by the day. As they grew, so did Arafat's sense of his own power. He was developing important plans for al-Fatah.

Ahmed El Shukairy, seen here addressing people in Gaza, was the head of the Palestinian Liberation Organization before Arafat took over.

4

From al-Fatah Member to PLO Leader: 1963-1969

A l-Fatah responsibilities soon took over all aspects of Arafat's life. He was no longer working as an engineer in Kuwait. His role in al-Fatah had become his full-time job. He watched carefully as Nasser continued to complicate his life and the role of al-Fatah in the Palestinian world.

In 1964, the Arab League founded an organization that they named the Palestinian Liberation Organization (PLO). The Arab League was a voluntary association of independent, Arabic-speaking countries. The League had been formed in 1945 and was based in Cairo, Egypt. Its official goals were to bring together its member states, consolidate their strategies, and promote their shared well-being. It was to do all this while still allowing each nation/member to retain its own sovereignty.

The PLO was originally the idea of Egyptian President Gamal Abdul Nasser. Nasser wanted a group that would further unite the Arab world. By rallying the Arab states and people around the cause of liberating the Palestinians, Nasser hoped to gain greater control over all Arabic-speaking nations and especially over the Palestinian refugees. There is no doubt that Nasser must have also wanted to crush Arafat and al-Fatah's growing political power in the Arab world.

In January of 1964, the Arab leaders gathered in Cairo for the first Arab summit conference. At this time, the League was comprised of the nations of Egypt, Iraq, Saudi Arabia, Syria, Transjordan (Jordan, as of 1949), Yemen, Algeria, Kuwait, Libya, Morocco, and Tunisia. They voted not only to set up the PLO, but also to place Ahmad Shukeiri at its head. Ahmad Shukeiri was a Palestinian diplomat who was an official of the Arab League.

In May of that same year, the PLO gathered at the National Hotel in the section of Jerusalem that was under Jordanian control. There it issued a National Covenant that announced its advocacy of armed struggle. At this time, it also identified itself as being the official representative of the Palestinian people.

Abu Jihad and a delegation of al-Fatah members had attended the PLO meeting in Jerusalem, but Arafat was not among them. This way, al-Fatah could observe the PLO's actions while remaining uncommitted to their cause. Without Arafat's attendance or consent, al-Fatah could not pledge itself to the PLO. This was a shrewd action on the part of Arafat and al-Fatah because the PLO wanted to control al-Fatah. They could not, however, accuse al-Fatah members of refusing to join if Arafat was not in attendance to help make such a momentous decision. Thus, the members of al-Fatah were not openly opposed to the PLO, but nor were they embracing it.

Arafat's organization remained on its own. It did not pledge loyalty to the PLO. Arafat and the other head members of al-Fatah were not ready to join Nasser, who was the man who had once taken weapons away from irregular Palestinians and even imprisoned those who had wanted to continue the fight against Israel during the mid-1950s. Arafat and his closest associates neither liked nor trusted this man.

Arafat and al-Fatah were now facing a great political opponent. All of the major Arab nations backed the PLO. The PLO was claiming to be the official representative of the Palestinian people, and it had many more members and much more political clout than al-Fatah had. If it was to continue gaining Palestinian support, then, al-Fatah had to make the Palestinian people believe that al-Fatah, not the PLO, had the real interests of the Palestinian people at heart. Arafat had to keep the Arab nations happy, while reminding the Palestinians that their so-called Arab brothers had let them down in the past. Al-Fatah also had to increase its numbers and political power.

By 1965, al-Fatah was initiating attacks against Israel and raids of its territory. Arafat's commando activities with al-Fatah in 1966 created great difficulties for himself as well as his organization. Many of al-Fatah's members were arrested. Some turned against the group and became informants when they were caught; others died trying to carry out their missions. Arafat too was arrested at one point.

Arafat did not mind facing difficulties personally, as long as they were for the benefit of the Palestinian cause. He did not like facing difficulties, however, if they interfered with his dream of the creation of an independent Palestinian state. The PLO was interfering with this dream. Unlike the PLO's feelings toward him and al-Fatah, Arafat's feelings toward the PLO were kept secret.

Ahmad Shukairy, the chairman of the PLO, declared that

Arafat and his fellow al-Fatah members were enemies of the Palestinian Liberation Movement. In Jordan they were considered to be treacherous revolutionaries. The Saudis openly called them representatives of global communism. In Egypt, Nasser labeled al-Fatah members as being extreme fanatical tools of the Muslim Brotherhood.

Al-Fatah turned to Syria, and with the Syrians' help they launched raids from Jordan, Lebanon, and Gaza. Al-Fatah's underground military wing was to become known as Thunderstorm, or al-Assifa. Al-Fatah's first military action was an attempt to blow up the Israeli Mekorot Water Corporation, but this failed.

Arafat was arrested in May of 1966 for his part in a plot to explode a section of the Tapline pipe. The Tapline pipe was part of the Trans-Arabian Pipeline Company's pipeline that carried Saudi Arabian oil out to the Mediterranean Sea. This failed mission did not make al-Fatah any friends among the Arabs or the Syrians. The pipeline was a prized economic resource. Still, al-Fatah's attacks on Israel continued until the Six-Day War in June of 1967.

The Six-Day War dealt a tremendous blow to many Arabic-speaking nations and Palestinians. While Egypt, Syria, and Jordan were readying their troops for war, Israel learned of their plans and struck first. A massive air strike launched by Israel devastated the air forces of Egypt, Syria, and Jordan. After six days, the war ended with Israel taking command of Egypt's Gaza Strip, Syria's Golan Heights, and Jordan's West Bank, including the Old City of Jerusalem. This placed over 1.5 million Arabs under Israeli control.

The Six-Day War also offered al-Fatah a great opportunity. With Arabs and Palestinians alike embarrassed by their defeat, the call for pan-Arabic nationalism had lost its allure. Egypt's Nasser was no longer in a position to defame al-Fatah. If anything, the opposite was now true. It was time for al-Fatah to defame pan-Arabic nationalism.

Israeli soldiers celebrate at the holy Wailing Wall in Old Jerusalem after taking over the city during the 1967 Six-Day War.

Arafat recognized his chance. He quickly called a meeting of the leaders of al-Fatah in Damascus, Syria, on June 23, 1967. Here, they decided to continue their fight against Israel. With Arafat's support, they decided to head the fight from inside the territories that had been seized during the Six-Day War.

Arafat and his friends were shocked, along with the rest of the Arabic-speaking world, when on June 28, 1967, Israel announced that it was going to annex the Arab section of Jerusalem. Residents of the Magharba district of the old city were given twenty-four hours to leave their homes. The home of Arafat's Uncle Selim was torn down, along with the homes of many others.

Abu Jihad, Abu Iyad, and Arafat knew that al-Fatah's time had come. Palestinians everywhere were calling for a *jihad,* or holy war, and al-Fatah was the group that could organize and lead them. Above all else, al-Fatah had the creation of a Palestinian state and the good of the Palestinian people in mind.

Arafat sneaked over into the West Bank, eluding Israeli intelligence agents. In Ramallah and Nablus, he coordinated the activities of Palestinian activists. Unable to stay in one place for very long, he avoided detection by the Israeli police by hiding out in the underground cells that were already being organized.

Arafat spent about a month promoting al-Fatah and its beliefs to Palestinian refugees throughout the West Bank. During this month, he was constantly on the move. It was often necessary for him to wear disguises and forge documents to avoid the Israeli Intelligence Agency. Tales of his courage and craftiness were whispered among his people but not yet made public.

Arafat and al-Fatah continued to keep their political and philosophical distance from the Arab states. Al-Fatah really had no use for most of the Arab nations, which sought to keep the Palestinians and al-Fatah under strict control. These nations not only had failed to arm the Palestinians but had on many occasions taken away the few armaments the Palestinian warriors had managed to procure.

Arafat, Abu Iyad, and Abu Jihad kept their movement centered on the Palestinian people and their armed struggle.

The battle of Karameh took place on March 21, 1968. This decisive battle helped to shape both al-Fatah and Arafat's history. Following orders given to them by Arafat, al-Fatah's fighters stood up to the Israeli army. At least 28 Israelis were killed at Karameh, and approximately 90 more were wounded. When the Israelis fled, they left damaged tanks and other vehicles behind.

Soon it was common knowledge among the Palestinian refugees that at Karameh 15,000 members of the Israeli Defense Force had retreated rather than face the al-Fatah fedayeen.

Though al-Fatah's fighting forces had been aided by PLO guerrillas and the Jordanian army, the glory of this battle was not shared. It all fell upon Arafat and his al-Fatah fedayeen. The bravery displayed by Arafat and his friends earned them instant hero status among the Palestinians. When no one else had wanted to fight, Arafat had urged them to stand tall.

Arafat had practically shamed the PLO and Jordanian fighting forces into holding their ground by pledging that his forces would indeed stand their ground against the Israelis. As usual, Arafat stood out from the crowd. Even among the heroes of al-Fatah's forces, he was not just another hero. He was the hero in charge.

Striking while the iron was still hot, the members of al-Fatah immediately agreed that Arafat should now become their official spokesman. Arafat, and only Arafat, would publish announcements and issue statements in al-Fatah's name. The name Yasir Arafat would soon become synonymous with al-Fatah and the Palestinian struggle. Al-Fatah was readying Arafat to take center stage in the Middle East's ongoing drama.

The Palestinian refugees were now really hungry for organized leadership that the mismanaged PLO was not providing. With al-Fatah and Arafat already in possession of increasing public support, Arafat and his associates again saw a chance for the advancement of their movement. The PLO's weakness was to become an advantage for al-Fatah.

Yasir Arafat in 1969, not long after being elected Chairman of the PLO.

Al-Fatah joined the PLO in 1968, and by early February of 1969 Arafat had been elected chairman of the PLO. Under the leadership of Arafat, the PLO gained widespread support among Palestinians.

Once he took over as head of the PLO, Arafat's image and

name quickly became known throughout the Middle East and the rest of the world. Many people saw him as a heroic fedayeen dressed in a soldier's uniform. Many others saw him as a murderous terrorist, hiding beneath dark sunglasses and a long beard. To all who knew his name now, however, he was the head of the PLO. Arafat was known in many circles as "Mr. Palestine." His vision of the future was slowly coming to realization.

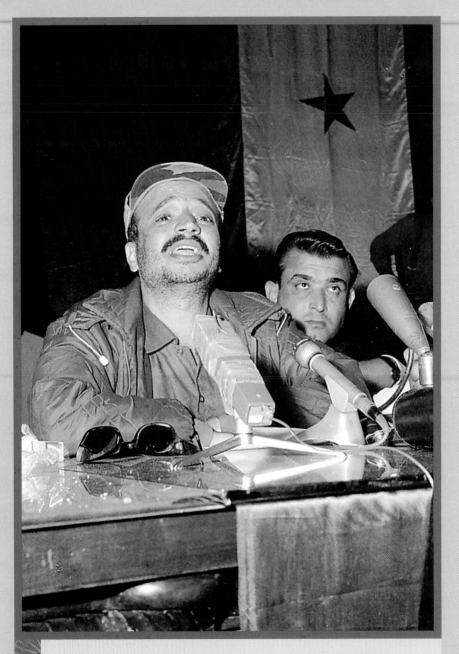

Arafat, shown here speaking at a 1969 press conference in Damascus, Syria, began to take a prominent role in Middle East politics by the late 1960s.

5

Black
September:
1969–1974

In the late 1960s and the early 1970s, Yasir Arafat and the PLO were based in Jordan. By early 1970, seven guerrilla organizations were also actively organizing strikes from within Jordan's borders. Although Arafat, who was now Chairman of the PLO, sought to combine these various guerrilla groups and control them, he was having little luck actually doing so.

King Hussein was providing the PLO and Arafat's fedayeen with training sites and other assistance. Living in refugee camps, Arafat and the fedayeen began to ignore King Hussein's authority, however. With their increased strength, due to arms and financial support from other nations in the Arab world and some within the Eastern European block, Arafat's troops were beginning to threaten the stability of Jordan.

With each guerilla attack waged against Israel, the threat to

Hussein's authority grew. King Hussein's Bedouin army tried to stop the PLO. Battles broke out between Arafat's fedayeen and the Jordanian army during the first half of 1970. In June of 1970, an Arab mediation committee intervened to halt two weeks of serious fighting between the two sides.

In June, King Hussein chose Abd al-Munim ar-Rifai to head a "reconciliation" cabinet and to meet with Arafat. On June 9, 1970, Rifai and Arafat signed an agreement that was highly favorable to Arafat and the fedayeen.

Arafat and his men were guaranteed freedom of movement within Jordan. Furthermore, he had obtained an agreement from Rifai that said Jordan would refrain from anti-guerrilla action. Finally, Jordan formally expressed its support for the fedayeen in the battle against Israel.

In return, Arafat pledged that he and his men would remove their bases from Amman, withdraw armed personnel from the Jordanian capital, and honor Jordanian law. The Popular Front for the Liberation of Palestine, or PFLP, headed by George Habash, effectively destroyed this agreement when they launched an airline hijacking campaign that shocked Jordan and the world.

In August of 1970, Arafat and his closest confidantes met in Amman. The meeting of the Palestine National Council had one primary purpose: the PLO was plotting to establish a completely separate Palestinian state with Arafat as its leader. Arafat, foolishly, did not believe that King Hussein would risk the wrath of other Arab nations by striking out against the Palestinians. Hussein was enraged when he heard rumors of this plan and of Arafat's bravado, and the tension between Hussein and the PLO grew stronger.

On September 6, a group of PFLP members hijacked a TWA jet and a Swissair jet, as well as attempting to seize control of an El Al plane. Later that same day, another PFLP group hijacked a Pan Am jet and forced the crew to fly to Beirut. The airliner was refueled and flown to Cairo. In Cairo,

Arafat and Jordanian Premier Abd al-Munim ar-Rifai walk hand in hand after signing an important treaty in 1970. Serious fighting between Jordanian soldiers and Arafat's fedayeen ended with the agreement, which was highly favorable to the Palestinian cause.

the passengers and crew were forced to evacuate the plane. It was then blown up. The PFLP hijackings were staged primarily to undermine the Jarring Peace Talks.

These actions did not help Arafat's already precarious standing in King Hussein's eyes, or the PLO's position in

Jordan, even though the PFLP was obviously beyond Arafat's control. King Hussein felt threatened once again by the anti-Israeli guerilla groups that existed within Jordan's borders.

On September 16, King Hussein placed Jordan under martial law. That same day, Arafat was named Commander in Chief of the Palestinian Liberation Army (PLA), the PLO's regular military force. Hussein and his militia immediately ordered the fedayeen to lay down their arms and to evacuate all of Jordan's cities. Arafat and the fedayeen refused, resulting in a war that lasted ten days. The small PLA fought the larger Jordanian Army tenaciously. Syria backed Arafat and sent about 200 tanks to aid the fedayeen.

On September 22, 1970, an Arab League Delegation arrived in Amman, Jordan. Arafat was still on the run, but PLO leaders Abu Iyad and Farouk Qaddoumi had been captured. King Hussein released them so that they might work together to reach a peace accord with the help of the Arab League.

A tentative agreement was reached, and the Arab delegates flew back to Cairo. Arafat was not impressed, however. He rejected the agreement and publicly called for an overthrow of King Hussein and the Jordanian government.

Next, Arafat was asked to travel to Cairo for a peace talk. Both Arafat and Hussein arrived in Cairo wearing military garb and carrying firearms. Neither appeared ready to reach a peaceful settlement to their problems. The Arab League finally managed, after much work, to persuade the two men to leave their firearms out of the peace negotiations.

Hussein and Arafat argued loudly. Arafat told Hussein that he was an imperialist traitor, loyal to Israel and the United States. He accused Hussein of plotting against the people of Palestine. He screamed. He yelled. He pounded his fists. King Hussein responded by angrily screaming back at Arafat. Hussein accused Arafat of planning to overthrow the Crown and of repaying Jordan's help with treachery. Arafat, in turn, said Hussein was a pawn of the United States and Israel.

The insults flew back and forth between the two men, until Egyptian President Nasser finally had enough. A talented states-man, Nasser put an end to the aggression, skillfully guiding the two opposing Arabs to reach an agreement. Grudgingly, Arafat and Hussein shook hands and adopted a peace agreement.

President Nasser collapsed several hours later, suffering a heart attack, and died. Anwar Sadat would soon take control of the Egyptian government. Sadat would not be as willing to help Arafat as his predecessor had been. Arafat mourned the loss of Nasser, despite the differences that they had had in the past. Without Nasser, it seemed the Cairo Agreement was doomed to fail.

The Cairo Agreement called for a swift departure of Arafat's guerrilla forces from all Jordanian cities and towns. The guerillas would be allowed to occupy only positions necessary for contin-uing the battle with Israel. Both sides were to release prisoners taken over the course of the ten-day war. Things did not go according to the late Nasser's plans, however.

On October 13, 1970, King Hussein and Arafat met again. This time they signed an agreement in Amman. The agreement stated that the fedayeen would recognize Jordanian sovereignty and the king's authority. It further stipulated that the guerillas would remove their armed forces from towns and villages, and stop carrying arms outside their camps. In return, Arafat and the fedayeen were granted amnesty for incidents that had occurred during the civil war. The agreement was signed, but fighting still broke out sporadically between the fedayeen and Jordan's military forces.

The last few months of 1970, as well as the first six months of 1971, were marked by a series of broken peace accords between Hussein and Arafat. The battles between the fedayeen and the Jordanian army continued. The Jordanian army pushed forward in an attempt to remove the fedayeen from populated regions within its borders.

The fedayeen finally withdrew from Amman in April of 1971. Feeling threatened by Hussein, the Arafat-led al-Fatah

To arm themselves in their struggle, the Palestinians have resorted to gun smuggling. Here, security forces examine illegal guns and ammunition at an al-Widhat refugee camp in Jordan.

organization completely and quite vocally abandoned its earlier posture of noninvolvement in the internal affairs of an Arab state. Arafat and al-Fatah began to publicly demand the over-throw of the Jordanian government.

King Hussein ordered his forces to attack the lingering guerrillas throughout Jordan. His Bedouin army struck swiftly and mercilessly against Arafat's militia.

Around mid-July, the Jordanian army marched against the

PLO's fedayeen bases that were located northwest of Amman in the Ajlun area. Arafat's last camps were in serious danger. Jordan also repealed the Cairo and Amman agreements at this time. No longer would they be bound by the recent agreements signed by Hussein and Arafat. Arafat and his fedayeen were a threat to Jordan and would not be tolerated or respected.

By late in July, King Hussein's government announced to the world that the remainder of the fedayeen bases in northern Jordan had been destroyed. More than 2,300 of the 2,500 fedayeen were arrested by Jordan's army. Many others fled the country.

For Arafat it had also become apparent that it was time to flee the country. Traveling with the Saudi ambassador to Jordan, at first it appeared that Arafat was going to meet with King Hussein. Apparently, he changed his mind somewhere around Jarresh, Jordan. At this point in the journey toward King Hussein's palace, Arafat asked to be taken to the Syrian border instead of to the scheduled meeting with King Hussein.

Arafat's escape from Jordan spawned many rumors. He was already known to be a master of disguise, having evaded detection by the Israeli forces time and time again, and many say he disappeared in Jordan by dressing up as an old woman and walking right past Jordanian soldiers and into Syria.

No matter how he was dressed or how he got there, Arafat arrived safe in Lebanon. Almost immediately, he assembled over two thousand men. As Chairman of the PLO and Commander in Chief of the PLA, Arafat was ready to begin business as usual in a new base camp: Lebanon.

In November of 1971, an al-Fatah Convention was called to examine what had gone wrong in Jordan between King Hussein's government and the Palestinian fedayeen forces. Arafat reportedly stormed in and out of the meeting several times. He refused to accept any blame for the problems that had occurred between himself and King Hussein. Instead, he blamed his longtime friends Abu Iyad and Abu Jihad. He was angry with them both. Abu Iyad had signed a peace treaty with

Hussein without Arafat's knowledge or permission. Abu Jihad had simply chastised fedayeen behavior in Jordan and called for all PLO members to give King Hussein more respect.

In essence, each of his friends had challenged Arafat's authority to some degree, and Arafat did not like to be challenged by anyone. So, a self-righteous Arafat, unwilling to accept any blame for his actions, placed the Jordan disaster squarely on the shoulders of these two prominent members of al-Fatah. Arafat was above reproach in his own eyes. He was, after all, the symbol of Palestine.

Although a majority of the members of al-Fatah were not happy with Arafat's behavior, Jordan soon managed to deflect their anger back onto itself. The Jordanians were treating the Palestinians of the West Bank and Gaza camps very poorly, and sentiment throughout the Middle East was turning back to the side of the Palestinians. Anti-Hussein emotions were running high throughout the Arab world in general. The Palestinians, in particular, were extremely angry with Hussein at this time.

Arafat knew he needed to make the most of all of these feelings. He railed against Jordan's treachery. He publicly chastised the Arab nations for their lack of support for the Palestinian people. He pointed his finger at Israel and denounced their occupation of Palestinian territory over and over again in a loud voice aimed at the ears, hearts, and minds of the Palestinian people. The PLO leader averred that it was time for the Palestinians to come together. Arafat capitalized on the mistakes of the Jordanians, the lack of support from other Arab nations, and the pain of the people of Palestine to gather support for himself and his PLO.

For the next several years, Arafat and the PLO staged attacks upon northern Israel from fedayeen bases in Lebanon. A terrorist group calling itself Black September began waging strikes against various political targets. Many experts believe that Arafat merely created Black September to distance himself and the PLO from the political backlash associated with acts of terrorism.

The Black September Organization (BSO) carried out numerous acts of terrorism from approximately 1971 to 1974. The first reported assassination mission carried out by Black September took place on November 28, 1971, when the group gunned down Jordan's Prime Minister, Wasif Tel. Ever aware of the power of world opinion, the politically shrewd Arafat publicly denied any connection to the group.

One of Black September's most infamous attacks took place on September 5, 1972, at the Munich Olympics. The Arab terrorists demanded that approximately two hundred political prisoners be released. In the resulting confrontation, eleven Israeli athletes, five terrorists, and a policeman were slain. The world reacted with horror, vilifying Arafat for his alleged involvement in the Munich massacre.

Did Arafat order the massacre? Probably not. The PLO's longtime foreign affairs spokesman, Khalid al-Hassan, had been completely against terrorism. In fact, he resigned in reaction to Black September's assassination of Israeli Prime Minister Tel. Unlike Spokesman Hassan, however, Abu Iyad, Abu Jihad, Kamal Adwan, Abu Hassan, and George Habash fully supported the use of terrorism to achieve their goals. During arguments between the more hawkish members of the PLO and the less militant al-Hassan, Arafat walked the middle ground.

Arafat, as usual, did not want to lose support from either side, so the Palestinian leader merely qualified that any acts of terrorism should not be undertaken in the name of the PLO. He did not want to shoulder the responsibility or political backlash for terrorism. It is very unlikely, however, that he ordered a stop to all acts of terrorism

On the other hand, there is no clear proof that suggests Arafat ordered any of the acts of terrorism that were carried out by Black September. Black September did, however, fall under the umbrella of the PLO. This meant that at the time of the Munich Massacre, Arafat, as head of the PLO, was also the head of Black September. As such, he most likely could have put a stop to the group's actions had he chosen to do so.

It was an attack against an Arab embassy that forced Arafat to take action against Black September. On March 1, 1973, a Black September hit squad forced its way into the Saudi Embassy in Khartoum, Sudan. Inside the embassy, the eight-man hit team interrupted a farewell party for an American charge d'affaires, J. Curtis Moore. The hit team held hostages at gun point and demanded the release of Palestinian political prisoners.

This time, in Arafat's opinion, Black September had gone too far. The group was risking incurring the wrath of the United States, insulting the President of Sudan, and spitting in the face of the Saudis. President Numeiri of Sudan had saved Arafat during a conflict in Amman, the Saudis were financially supportive of the PLO, and the United States was a superpower that the PLO Chairman did not want to battle. Arafat was incensed by the stupidity of this latest act of terrorism, and he ordered an end to all acts of terrorism.

The violence continued, however, since Arafat was not in control of all of the radical splinter groups that claimed to be representatives of the Palestinian people. Arafat was unwilling to use military force to stop terrorism for fear that Palestinians would view this as a traitorous act, so his hands were tied. Therefore, he began secretly working toward reaching a peaceful agreement with the Israelis.

Arafat could not, at this time, openly acknowledge to the people of Palestine that he was seeking an end to their armed struggle. The Palestinians were not ready for such an announcement. He had promised the Palestinians that he would lead them back to their homeland. He had promised them a nation of their own. If he made any concessions to the Israelis, the Palestinian people would never support or forgive him. Arafat could not face such a prospect.

In 1973, radical Black September guerrillas killed two Americans at the Saudi Arabian embassy in Khartoum. Arafat, fearing this would provoke the United States, immediately condemned the act.

Chairman Arafat would not allow himself to lose the respect or support of the Palestinian people. It was imperative that he remain in control. For personal and political reasons, Arafat could not allow himself to lose his status as the "Father of Palestine." He was "the old man." He was "Mr. Palestine." He was determined to remain all of those things in the eyes of his people and in the chronicles of history.

On October 6, 1973, the Egyptian and Syrian armies moved across the Suez Canal and attacked the Golan Heights. The Palestinian Army fought alongside the Egyptians and Syrians. Four days after the fighting began, Arafat sent a peace message to U.S. Secretary of State Henry Kissinger. Not only did Kissinger not reply to Arafat's message expressing a willingness to work for peace, but when Kissinger arranged for a peace conference to be held in Geneva he did not even invite the PLO. Instead, he invited Egyptian President Anwar Sadat and Syrian President Hafez Assad.

Not wanting to appear less powerful or influential in the situation, Arafat began politicking for peace. Israel was not pleased with the international support this began to win Arafat, but Kissinger seemed content to ignore Arafat and to dismiss the PLO as a terrorist organization.

The PLO suffered a great deal of internal disharmony during this time. George Habash and his PFLP formed a group that became known as the Rejectionist Front, which rejected Arafat's decision to discard the tactic of armed struggle and replace it with peaceful negotiation. Arafat's eyes were on gaining recognition from the United States, however, and he determinedly pushed forward.

On October 26, 1974, an Arab summit was held in Rabat, Morocco. Arafat left the summit joyous; the summit had not only confirmed steps taken earlier at a summit in Algiers, but it also had accepted the PLO and, in essence, Arafat as the only valid representative of the Palestine people. Furthermore, the summit announced that the Arab leaders believed that the PLO should establish and be the head of the Palestinian national government in any and all areas of a liberated Palestine.

Arafat was overjoyed. Henry Kissinger was not. Despite Israel and the United States' reluctance to deal with Arafat and the Palestinians, the United Nations moved to add another feather to Arafat's cap. With dissent only from the United States

Arafat in 1974, the same year he made his landmark address to the United Nations in New York City.

and Israel, the United Nations invited Arafat to address its General Assembly.

For Arafat and the Palestinian people, hope sprang anew. The world was recognizing them as a legitimate entity. Arafat saw a chance for peace and the establishment of a free Palestinian nation. Mr. Palestine had come a long, long way, and he proudly brought his people along with him.

Arafat addresses the United Nations General Assembly on November 13, 1974. The speech was a groundbreaking moment for the PLO leader, who felt that his dreams for a free Palestine were finally being listened to by the international community.

6

At Last a Voice:
November 13, 1974

I n 1974, the United Nations (U.N.) voted to give the PLO observer status. The U.N. also declared that the Palestinians had a right to self-determination. Arafat was jubilant. Palestine's time had finally come.

To the world at large, Arafat seemed very willing to work towards a political settlement with the Israelis. Peace in the Middle East seemed more possible than ever. Still, Henry Kissinger and the Israeli government were not very willing to work with Arafat.

A determined Arafat addressed the U.N. in New York on November 13, 1974. Legend has it that he stood before the U.N. holding an olive branch and carrying a gun. In reality, he held an olive branch and wore an empty holster. He was dressed in his now characteristic olive-green military attire.

Arafat directed his opening remarks to the U.N.'s president and its secretary general. He began by congratulating Guinea-Bissau, Bangladesh, and Grenada on their recent acceptance into the U.N. and thanking the assembly in general for its support.

Arafat spoke for a while on the need for the United Nations to support countries and people faced with racial discrimination, oppression, imperialism, occupation, and aggression and talked of the political problems of Indo-China, Viet Nam, Laos, and Cyprus. He called for an end to "the siphoning off of the wealth of impoverished peoples," referring to a recently held United Nations Assembly meeting on raw materials and development.

Chairman Arafat then addressed the escalation of the arms race throughout the world: he called for the U.N. to work towards curbing the unnecessary buildup of nuclear arms and for the prevention of nuclear war. Only then did he really begin to speak about the state of Palestine.

At first, Arafat mentioned how his homeland had become the most stressful region in the world as "the Zionist entity clings tenaciously to occupied Arab territory; Zionism persists in its aggressions against us and our territory." He remarked on the world's need to work aggressively for the end of "colonialism, imperialism, neo-colonialism, and racism." Arafat held the belief that the world was in a state of "glorious change" in which "just causes" would succeed.

At that point, Arafat really began to plead his case. The Palestinian leader led this section of his speech with some general remarks about the question of Palestine. Next, he launched into a long and passionate discourse on what he viewed as the Jewish invasion of Palestine. This section of his dialogue began with the Jewish immigrations of 1881 into Palestine and ended with the War of 1973, covering almost one hundred years of history.

When he was finished outlining his version of the years from 1881 to 1973, his voice grew louder and his speech more impassioned. Arafat wanted everyone in the room to remember this speech. He wanted all to hear what he had to say on the behalf of his beloved Palestine.

Mr. Palestine knew that this was, to date, his finest hour. Palestine's cause was finally getting the attention it deserved. He cleared his throat and spoke in a loud, controlled, and yet passionate voice:

It pains our people greatly to witness the propagation of the myth that its homeland was a desert until it was made to bloom by the toil of foreign settlers, that it was a land without a people, and that the colonialist entity caused no harm to any human being.

No. Such lies must be exposed from this rostrum, for the world must know that Palestine was the cradle of the most ancient cultures and civilizations. Its Arab people were engaged in farming and building, spreading culture throughout the land for thousands of years, setting an example in the practice of freedom of worship, acting as faithful guardians of the holy places of all religions. As a son of Jerusalem, I treasure for myself and my people beautiful memories and vivid images of the religious brotherhood that was the hallmark of our Holy City before it succumbed to catastrophe.

Our people continued to pursue this enlightened policy until the establishment of the State of Israel and their dispersion. This did not deter our people from pursuing their humanitarian role on Palestinian soil. Nor will they permit their land to become a launching pad for aggression or a racist camp predicated on the destruction of civilization, cultures, progress, and peace. Our people cannot but maintain the heritage of their ancestors in resisting the invaders, in assuming the privileged task of defending their native land, their Arab nationhood, their culture and civilization, and in safeguarding the cradle of monotheistic religion.

We need only mention briefly some Israeli stands: its support of the Secret Army Organization in Algeria, its bolstering of the settler-colonialists in Africa—whether in the Congo, Angola, Mozambique, Zimbabwe, Azania, or

South Africa—and its backing of South Vietnam against the Vietnamese revolution. In addition, how can we not mention Israel's continuing support of imperialists and racists everywhere, its obstructionist stand in the Committee of Twenty-Four, its refusal to cast its vote in support of independence for the African States, and its opposition to the demands of many Asian, African, and Latin American nations, and several other States in the conference on raw materials, population, the Law of the Sea, and food.

All these facts offer further proof of the character of the enemy which has usurped our land. They justify the honorable struggle which we are waging against it. As we defend a vision of the future, our enemy upholds the myths of the past.

The enemy we face has a long record of hostility even towards the Jews themselves, for there is within the Zionist entity a built-in racism against Oriental Jews. While we are vociferously condemning the massacres of Jews under Nazi rule, Zionist leadership appeared more interested at that time in exploiting them as best it could in order to realize its goal of immigration into Palestine.

If the immigration of Jews to Palestine had had as its objective the goal of enabling them to live side by side with us, enjoying the same rights and assuring the same duties, we would have opened our doors to them, as far as our homeland's capacity for absorption permitted. Such was the case with the thousands of Armenians and Circassians who still live among us in equality and brethren and citizens. But that the goal of this immigration should be to usurp our homeland, disperse our people, and turn us into second-class citizens—this is what no one can conceivably demand that we acquiesce in or submit to.

Arafat carefully sought to keep the international community from seeing him or his people as racists. He did this by explaining the Palestinian viewpoint on the difference between

Zionism and Judaism. Knowing that the fate of Palestine could be helped or hindered dramatically by world opinion, he clarified the motivations behind the Palestinian revolution:

> Therefore, since its inception, our revolution has not been motivated by racial or religious factors. Its target has never been the Jew, as a person, but racist Zionism and undisguised aggression. In this sense, ours is also a revolution for the Jew as a human being, as well. We are struggling so that Jews, Christians, and Muslims may live in equality, enjoying the same rights and assuming the same duties, free from racial or religious discrimination.
>
> We do distinguish between Judaism and Zionism. While we maintain our opposition to the colonialist Zionist movement, we respect the Jewish faith. Today, almost one century after the rise of the Zionist movement, we wish to warn of its increasing danger to the Jews of the world, to our Arab people, and to world peace and security. For Zionism encourages the Jew to emigrate out of his homeland and grants him an artificially created nationality. The Zionists proceed with their terrorist activities even though these have proved ineffective. The phenomenon of constant emigration from Israel, which is bound to grow as the bastions of colonialism and racism in the world fall, is an example of the inevitability of the failure of such activities.
>
> [...]
>
> Why should our Arab Palestinian people . . . be responsible for the problems of Jewish immigration, if such problems exist in the minds of some people? Why do not the supporters of these problems open their own countries, which can absorb and help these immigrants?

Arafat then deftly addressed the problem of language itself in the struggle between Israel and Palestine. Specifically, he talked about the use of the word *terrorists* to describe the PLO.

Jewish refugees disembark from the *Haviva Reik* at Haifa in 1946. Two years later, the Jewish people and the United Nations would create the state of Israel and realize the Zionist dream of a homeland. Arafat, in his 1974 speech to the U.N., noted the difference between Zionism, which he opposes, and Judaism, the religion that he feels should be tolerated by Palestinians.

He said the PLO was no more a terrorist group than any other group that had tried to escape the domination of someone else:

> Those who call us terrorists wish to prevent world public opinion from discovering the truth about us and from seeing the justice on our faces. They seek to hide the terrorism and tyranny of their acts, and our own posture of self-defense. The difference between the revolutionary and the terrorist lies in the reason for which each fights. For whoever stands by a just cause and fights for the freedom and liberation of his land from the invaders, the settlers and

the colonialists, cannot possibly be called terrorist, otherwise the American people in their struggle for liberation from the British colonialists would have been terrorists; the European resistance against the Nazis would be terrorism; the struggle of the Asian, African, and Latin American peoples would also be terrorism, and many of you who are in this Assembly hall would be considered terrorists.

Despite his address's many affirmations of the Palestinians' desire for peace and their total lack of vengeful feelings, Arafat did talk at length about the misdeeds of the Zionists, paradoxically using to describe them the same word, *terrorists*, that he denied could be applied negatively to the PLO:

> Zionist terrorism which was waged against the Palestinian people to evict it from its country and usurp its land is registered in our official documents. Thousands of our people were assassinated in their villages and towns; tens of thousands of others were forced at gunpoint to leave their homes and the lands of their fathers. Time and time again our children, women, and aged were evicted and had to wander in the deserts and climb mountains without any food or water. No one who in 1948 witnessed the catastrophe that befell the inhabitants of hundreds of villages and towns, in Jerusalem, Jaffa, Lydda, Ramle, and Galilee, no one who has been a witness to that catastrophe will ever forget the experience, even though the mass blackout has succeeded in hiding these horrors as it has hidden the traces of 385 Palestinian villages and towns destroyed at the time and erased from the map. The destruction of 19,000 houses during the past seven years, which is equivalent to the complete destruction of two hundred more Palestinian villages, and the great number of maimed as a result of the treatment they were subjected to in Israeli prisons, cannot be hidden by any blackout.

[...]

For tens of years Zionists have been harassing our people's cultural, political, social, and artistic leaders, terrorizing them and assassinating them. They have stolen our cultural heritage, our popular folklore, and have claimed it as theirs. Their terrorism even reached our sacred places in our beloved and peaceful Jerusalem. They have endeavored to de-Arabize it and make it lose its Muslim and Christian character by evicting its inhabitants and annexing it.

[...]

The small number of Palestinian Arabs who were not uprooted by the Zionists in 1948 are at present refugees in their own homeland. Israeli law treats them as second-class citizens—and even as third-class citizens since Oriental Jews are second-class citizens—and they have been subject to all forms of racial discrimination and terrorism after confiscation of their land and property. They have been victims of bloody massacres such as that of Kfar Kassim, they have been expelled from their villages and denied the right to return, as in the case of the inhabitants of Rait and Kfar-Birim. For twenty-six years, our population has been living under martial law and was denied the freedom of movement without prior permission from the Israeli military governor, this at a time when an Israeli law was promulgated granting citizenship to any Jew anywhere who wanted to emigrate to our homeland. Moreover, another Israeli law stipulated that Palestinians who were not present in their villages or towns at the time of the occupation were not entitled to Israeli citizenship.

The record of Israeli rulers is replete with acts of terror perpetrated on those of our people who remained under occupation in Sinai and the Golan Heights. The criminal bombardment of the Bahr-al-Bakar School and the Abou Zaabal factory are but two such unforgettable acts of

When Israel became a state in 1948, armed conflict between
Palestinians and Israelis left almost half a million Palestinians
homeless, such as these refugees in Amman, Jordan.

terrorism. The total destruction of the Syrian city of
Kuneitra is yet another tangible instance of systematic
terrorism. If a record of Zionist terrorism in South Lebanon
were to be compiled, the enormity of its acts would shock
even the most hardened: piracy, bombardments, scorched-
earth, destruction of hundreds of homes, eviction of
civilians and the kidnapping of Lebanese citizens. This
clearly constitutes a violation of Lebanese sovereignty and is
in preparation for the diversion of the Litani River waters.

Need one remind this Assembly of the numerous
resolutions adopted by it condemning Israeli aggressions
committed against Arab countries, Israeli violations of
human rights and the articles of the Geneva Conventions, as

well as the resolutions pertaining to the annexation of the city of Jerusalem and its restoration to its former status?

The only description for these acts is that they are acts of barbarism and terrorism. And yet, the Zionist racists and colonialists have the temerity to describe the just struggle of our people as terror. Could there be a more flagrant distortion of truth than this? We ask those who usurped our land, who are committing murderous acts of terrorism against our people and are practicing racial discrimination more extensively than the racists of South Africa, we ask them to keep in mind the United Nations General Assembly resolution that called for the one-year suspension of the membership of the Government of South Africa from the United Nations. Such is the inevitable fate of every racist country that adopts the law of the jungle, usurps the homeland of others, and persists in oppression.

For the past thirty years, our people have had to struggle against British occupation and Zionist invasion, both of which had one intention: namely, the usurpation of our land. Six major revolts and tens of popular uprisings were staged to foil these attempts, so that our homeland might remain ours. Over thirty thousand martyrs, the equivalent in comparative terms of six million Americans, died in the process.

When the majority of the Palestinian people were uprooted from [their] homeland in 1948, the Palestinian struggle for self-determination continued under the most difficult conditions. We tried every possible means to continue our political struggle to attain our national rights, but to no avail. Meanwhile, we had to struggle for sheer existence. Even in exile we educated our children. This was all a part of trying to survive.

The Palestinian people produced thousands of physicians, lawyers, teachers, and scientists who actively participated in the development of the Arab countries bordering on their usurped homeland. They utilized their income to assist the young and aged among their people who remained in the refugee camps. They educated their younger sisters and brothers, supported their parents, and cared for their children. All along, the Palestinian dreamed of return. Neither the Palestinian's allegiance to Palestine nor his determination to return waned; nothing could persuade him to relinquish his Palestinian identity or to forsake his homeland. The passage of time did not make him forget, as some hoped he would. When our people lost faith in the international community which persisted in ignoring its rights, and when it became obvious that the Palestinians would not recuperate one inch of Palestine through exclusively political means, our people had no choice but to resort to armed struggle. Into that struggle it poured its material and human resources. We bravely faced the most vicious acts of Israeli terrorism which were aimed at diverting our struggle and arresting it.

In the past ten years of our struggle, thousands of martyrs and twice as many wounded, maimed, and imprisoned were offered in sacrifice; all in an effort to resist the imminent threat of liquidation, to regain our right to self-determination and our undisputed right to return to our homeland. With the utmost dignity and the most admirable revolutionary spirit, our Palestinian people have not lost their spirit in Israeli prisons and concentration camps or when faced with all forms of harassment and intimidation. They struggle for sheer existence and they continue to strive to preserve the Arab character of their land. Thus it resists oppression, tyranny, and terrorism in their ugliest forms.

It is through our popular armed struggle that our political leadership and our national institutions finally crystallized and a national liberation movement, comprising all the Palestinian factions, organizations, and capabilities, materialized in the Palestine Liberation Organization.

Through our militant Palestine national liberation movement, our people's struggle matured and grew enough

PLO soldiers stand guard at headquarters in Chtaura, Lebanon.

to accommodate political and social struggle in addition to armed struggle. The Palestine Liberation Organization was a major factor in creating a new Palestinian individual, qualified to shape the future of our Palestine, not merely content with mobilizing the Palestinians for the challenges of the present.

The champion of the Palestinian people took time to praise his people for their cultural and educational successes, despite their circumstances. He applauded his people's enduring efforts to improve and maintain their heritage and culture. He also lambasted the Zionists for trying to destroy the Palestinian culture:

> The Palestine Liberation Organization can be proud of having a large number of cultural and educational activities, even while engaged in armed struggle, and at a time when it faced increasingly vicious blows of Zionist terrorism. We established institutes for scientific research, agricultural development, and

social welfare, as well as centers for the revival of our cultural heritage and the preservation of our folklore. Many Palestinian poets, artists, and writers have enriched Arab culture in partic- ular, and world culture generally. Their profoundly humane works have won the admiration of all those familiar with them. In contrast to that, our enemy has been systematically destroying our culture and disseminating, racist, imperialist ideologies, in short, everything that impedes progress, justice, democracy, and peace.

The next few moments of Arafat's speech emphasized the legitimacy of the PLO:

The Palestine Liberation Organization has earned its legitimacy because of the sacrifice inherent in its pioneer- ing role, and because of its dedicated leadership of the struggle. It has also been granted this legitimacy by the Palestinian masses, which in harmony with it have chosen it to lead the struggle according to its directives. The Palestine Liberation Organization has also gained its legitimization by representing every faction, union, or group as well as every Palestinian talent, either in the National Council or in people's institutions. This legitimacy was further strengthened by the support of the entire Arab nation, and it was consecrated during the last Arab Summit Conference, which reiterated the right of the Palestine Liberation Organization in its capacity as the sole representative of the Palestinian People, to establish an independent national State on all liberated Palestinian territory.

An important goal of this speech seems to have been to portray the Palestinian cause, and the PLO itself, as a friend to the world community, to stop the world's other nations from seeing the Palestinians as a people bent on terrorism to get what they wanted. Arafat stressed both the hardships that the

Palestinian people had faced since 1948 *and* the sympathy they felt for the persecuted Jews:

> For many years now, our people have been exposed to the ravages of war, destruction, and dispersion. It has paid in the blood of its sons that which cannot ever be compensated. It has borne the burdens of occupation, dispersion, eviction, and terror more uninterruptedly than any other people. And yet all this has made our people neither vindictive nor vengeful. Nor has it caused us to resort to the racism of our enemies. Nor have we lost the true method by which friend and foe are distinguished. For we deplore all those crimes committed against the Jews; we also deplore all the real discrimination suffered by them because of their faith.
>
> I am a rebel, and freedom is my cause. I know well that many of you present here today once stood in exactly the same resistance position as I now occupy and from which I must fight. You once had to convert dreams into reality by your struggle. Therefore you must now share my dream. I think this is exactly why I can ask you now to help, as together we bring out our dream into a bright reality, our common dream for a peaceful future in Palestine's sacred land.

Arafat then cited two examples of the revolutionary spirit, placing himself in the same context of fighting for the greater good that others had occupied before him. His language emphasized the abstract; he talked not of guns, bombs, tanks, and ruins, but rather of hopes and dreams, of a vision of the future of relief from the bloodshed of the present:

> Why therefore should I not dream and hope? For is not revolution the making real of dreams and hopes? So let us work together that my dream may be fulfilled, that I may return with my people out of exile, there in Palestine to live with this Jewish freedom-fighter and his partners, with this Arab priest and his brothers, in one democratic State where

Christian, Jew, and Muslim live in justice, equality, fraternity and progress.

Is this not a noble dream worthy of my struggle alongside all lovers of freedom everywhere? For the most admirable dimension of this dream is that it is Palestinian, a dream from out of the land of peace, the land of martyrdom and heroism, and the land of history, too.

Let us remember that the Jews of Europe and the United States have been known to lead the struggles for secularism and the separation of Church and State. They have also been known to fight against discrimination on religious grounds. How then can they continue to support the most fanatic, discriminatory, and closed of nations in its policy?

Arafat then sought to reduce the tensions between his beliefs and his opponents' beliefs by grouping himself with the Jews already living in Palestine against Zionism and the leaders of Israel, claiming to propose an inclusive peace:

> We invite them to emerge from their moral isolation into a more open realm of free choice. . . . We offer them the most generous solution, that we might live together in a framework of just peace in our democratic Palestine.

In a stance some might consider hypocritical—contrary to his actions—Arafat contended that he wished ardently for peace—but only a peace established under certain conditions:

> . . . [W]e do not wish one drop of either Arab or Jewish [blood] to be shed; neither do we delight in the continuation of killing, which would end once a just peace [has been achieved], based on what our people's rights, hopes, and aspirations [have] been.

He asked his audience and, more generally, the listening world to help Palestine to achieve its goal of reunion with its former lands for the greater good of the world community. The talents of the Palestinian people, he declared, were being

During his famous 1974 speech to the United Nations, Arafat declared, "I have come bearing an olive branch and a freedom fighter's gun. Do not let the olive branch fall from my hand."

wasted, their energies absorbed by the fight to regain what they never should have lost:

> . . . I appeal to you to accompany our people in their struggle to attain their right to self-determination. . . . I appeal to you, further, to aid our people's return to their homeland from an involuntary exile imposed upon them by force of arms, by tyranny, by oppression, so that we may regain our property, our land, and thereafter live in our national homeland, free

and sovereign, enjoying all the privileges of nationhood. Only then can we pour all our resources into the mainstream of human civilization. Only then can Palestinian creativity be concentrated on the service of humanity. Only then will our Jerusalem resume its historic role as a peaceful shrine for all religions. I appeal to you to enable our people to establish national independent sovereignty over its own land.

Arafat concluded his speech with what are now infamous words: "Today I have come bearing an olive branch and a freedom fighter's gun. Do not let the olive branch fall from my hand. I repeat: Do not let the olive branch fall from my hand."

Unfortunately, Arafat and his Palestinians and Israel and her Jews would be exchanging gunfire and olive branches for many years to come. The struggle for peace in the Middle East was far from over. Arafat had brought his people quite far, but their journey toward liberation was only beginning. Much gunfire and many olive branches had yet to be exchanged between the Palestinians and the Israelis.

Arafat addresses the Palestine Revolution Military Academy in Beirut, Lebanon, in 1978. During his speech, he asserted that the fight would continue "as long as there are Palestinian women who beget children."

7

Lebanon, the Intifada, and the Nobel Peace Prize

"I married a myth, but the marriage helped him step down
from his pedestal and become a human being."
—SUHA ARAFAT

Arafat's appearance before the United Nations did not warm
relations between the Palestinians and the Israelis as Arafat had
hoped. The United States and Israel still wanted to negotiate
with Jordan, rather than with Arafat and the PLO. Israel continued to
refuse to acknowledge the PLO, much to Arafat's chagrin.

Arafat did not have much time to focus on this political snub
backed by the United States, however. He had matters to attend to in
Beirut, Lebanon.

Lebanon's various Muslim groups were growing more and
more dissatisfied with the 1943 National Pact. The Pact had given

a dominant political role to a group of Lebanon's Christians, the Phalangists, much to the disapproval of the Muslims. Tensions were mounting quickly within the area.

Adding to these tensions were the many Palestinian Muslims, loyal to Arafat and the PLO, living in Lebanon. In southern Lebanon, Arafat had established a number of PLO bases, which made attacks on Israel tactically convenient.

The Lebanese Muslims aligned themselves politically with the PLO. On April 13, 1975, Phalangists commandeered a bus carrying many Palestinians. The passengers were slain, triggering a civil war between the Muslims and Christians of Lebanon.

In early 1976, the PLO joined the side of the Muslims after Christians attacked a Palestinian refugee camp. Israel supported the Christians, supplying them with arms. Syria sent 30,000 troops in an attempt to restore order in Lebanon and to realize a plan for peace.

By 1977, Lebanon was divided into a northern section, controlled by Syrian forces, and a coastal section controlled by the Christian forces. In southern Lebanon, there were small pockets of land dominated by both the leftist Muslims and the PLO. The Syrians opened fire on (shelled) a Christian stronghold in Beirut.

Israeli troops invaded southern Lebanon on March 14, 1978. Their goal was to eradicate all PLO bases. They began a military occupation from southern Lebanon to the Litani River. The U.N., however, demanded that the Israelis withdraw all troops from the area, which was then under the control of a U.N.-controlled peacekeeping force.

By 1980, though, Israeli jets were attacking the Syrians and bombing areas of Beirut. These attacks were acts of retribution against Arafat's PLO for rocket attacks that were launched by the PLO from Lebanon into northern Israel. A short-lived ceasefire went into effect on July 24, 1981. Intent on destroying the PLO, Israeli troops marched into the suburbs of Beirut

The Israelis attacked Lebanon in 1982, damaging buildings such as these at the Arab University in West Beirut. Arafat, seen here inspecting the site, moved his headquarters to Tunisia soon after.

and began an evacuation of PLO guerrillas in 1982.

In August of 1982, U.S. arbitration resulted in the evacuation of Syrian troops and PLO fighters from Beirut. The agreement also called for a multinational peacekeeping force comprised of U.S. Marines, along with French and

Italian units. This force was to patrol the region and keep the peace in the name of the U.N.

The Israeli-backed president, Bashir Gemayel, was elected to serve as head of Lebanon. Shortly afterwards, on September 14, he was assassinated. Israeli troops almost immediately crossed into West Beirut to secure Muslim militia strongholds. The Israeli forces allowed Lebanese Christian militias to massacre almost eight hundred Palestinian civilians in the refugee camps of Sabra and Shatila.

Shocked, angered, and saddened, Arafat held Israeli Minister of Defense Ariel Sharon responsible for the massacre. Sharon was held indirectly responsible by the Kahane Commission. The Palestinian people were outraged.

Arafat and his loyal PLO militia were in Tripoli. At this time, Arafat was fighting a sort of civil war of his own. PLO dissidents, supported by Syria, battled against Arafat and his troops for six long, bloody weeks. Arafat, again, led his men and fought beside them bravely. Finally, however, Arafat and his men were forced to evacuate.

On December 20, 1983, the Chairman of the Executive Committee of the PLO, and the Commander of the PLA, General Yasir Arafat left Tripoli with 1,000 militia members, aboard several Greek ships. The U.N., in an unprecedented show of support, allowed the Greek ships to fly U.N. flags.

Arafat moved his headquarters to Tunis, Tunisia. After suffering this severe defeat, he resiliently forged ahead. On October 1, 1985, Israeli planes bombed Arafat's Palestinian Liberation Organization headquarters in Tunis, but Arafat was unharmed and the attack served merely to add to the Palestinian people's reverence for their leader. Arafat was, in their eyes, invincible. While his headquarters might be bombed and militia members might fall to enemy bullets during the thick of battle, Arafat seemed to always emerge from such circumstances unscathed. Arafat, like Palestine, would never accept defeat at the hands of the Israelis.

To Israel's disgust, Arafat had not only avoided assassination but also turned the attempt upon his life into a publicity coup. The botched attack had provided the sly politician with yet another means of evoking the world's sympathy and bolstering Palestinian pride.

Nevertheless, this Palestinian pride was suffering. The people were tired of waiting for change. Twenty years after the Six-Day War of 1967, in December of 1987, an uprising broke out in Palestine, one known since as an *Intifada*—an Arabic word that means a sudden awakening from sleep or a state of unawareness. It also is used to refer to the shaking off of an unpleasant feeling. Politically, the word has come to be used as a name for the Palestinian rebellion against Israeli occupation.

The 1987 uprising began in the Gaza Strip. Word had spread throughout the strip that a fatal traffic collision had been caused by Israeli security service agents in retaliation for the stabbing of an Israeli the previous week. Teenagers armed with stones and slingshots quickly took to the streets. Arafat watched in dismay as the children of Palestine, armed with little more than stones, began battling the forces of the Israeli Defense Force. He was quick to express his support for the West Bank uprising.

In December of 1988, Arafat led the Palestine National Council in renouncing terrorism. Arafat and the PLO publicly acknowledged Israel's right to exist. In response, the United States began to openly initiate peace dialogues with Arafat and the PLO. For the first time in 13 years, the United States was formally communicating with Arafat.

In 1990, Arafat's personal life took a dramatic turn. The leader who had many times declared himself "married to Palestine," secretly married a woman named Suha Tawil. Suha and Arafat first met when she was working as a freelance journalist. Arafat's marriage to Suha was a shock to the Palestinian people because she is the daughter of a

Arafat with his wife and daughter, Suha and Zahwa. Many Palestinians were shocked when their leader married Suha, who is from a Christian family, and they have criticized her for spending much of her time in Paris. However, Suha has converted to Islam and has begun to win over the Palestinians for her unwavering support of their cause.

Christian family. Suha spent her first years of life in Nablus and then moved with her family to Ramallah. Her father was a banker; her mother, Raymonda Tawil, was a famous pro-PLO journalist who had spent a great deal of time under house arrest imposed by the Israelis.

Suha converted to the Muslim faith, but she remains to

this day very grounded in her adherence to the tenets of the Christian faith. Thirty-four years younger than her husband, she divides her time between Paris and Palestine. She is committed to the Palestinian people and to her husband's cause.

Although the Palestinian people at first condemned her for staying in Paris throughout most of the Intifada, Suha remained committed to her husband and to the Palestinian people. Slowly but surely, her modest lifestyle and sincere interest in the people living in poverty in the refugee camps has won her the support of the majority of Palestinians. She is not, however, always supportive of or supported by Arafat's government officials.

Arafat's closest advisors and friends seemed to be mystified by the relationship. Suha, a blonde woman not of clear Middle Eastern descent, was an enigma to them. Perhaps this is fitting, however, for Arafat has long been called an enigma in both political and journalistic circles throughout the world. His marriage to Suha only adds to the riddle that is Arafat.

Arafat made a crucial mistake in 1990. His support of Saddam Hussein's invasion of Kuwait was a political blunder that Palestine paid for dearly. The Persian Gulf states responded to Palestine's involvement by discontinuing their financial support of the Palestinian cause in general and the PLO in particular. When Iraq was defeated in the ensuing war, Arafat found himself in trouble, both politically and financially.

By 1993, Arafat and Israel's Yitzhak Rabin had established a peace agreement that provided for the gradual withdrawal of Israeli troops from the Gaza Strip and West Bank. The Palestinian Authority was also created under the 1993 peace agreements known as the Oslo Accords.

The year 1994 was marked by great activity and success in Arafat's life. In May of 1994, Israeli troops withdrew from Jericho. Just a few months later, in July, Arafat returned triumphantly to Palestine. On December 10, he gave a speech

Arafat receives his Nobel Peace Price in Oslo, Norway, in 1994, along with Israeli Prime Minister Yitzhak Rabin (right), and Israeli Foreign Minister Shimon Peres (center).

in acceptance of the Nobel Peace Prize. After his "gun and olive branch" speech, it was to be his most important oration to date.

The Palestinian Authority's legislative body, the 88-seat Palestinian Council, was elected in January of 1996. Arafat won a landslide victory as its president. The people of Palestine had spoken: Arafat was not only their hero; he was their chosen leader.

A few years later, Suha Arafat gave birth to a daughter; the couple named the child Zahwa, in honor of Arafat's long-deceased mother. The father of the Palestinian people was now the father of a little girl of his own.

Attending the Middle East Summit, in October of 2000, with Israeli Prime Minister Ehud Barak (left) and U.S. President Bill Clinton (center). Although the Israeli and Palestinian leaders promised to seek peace, fighting has continued.

8

A Cell Phone and a Submachine Gun: March–April 2002

> "They want me under arrest or in exile or dead,
> but I am telling them, I prefer to be martyred."
> —YASIR ARAFAT

I n the years between 1996 and 2000, it appeared for the most part that negotiations had taken the place of armed struggle in Arafat's life. However, something went dreadfully wrong at Camp David during the summer of 2000. Not only did Arafat refuse to accept the latest Israeli proposal for a Palestinian state, he left the peace talks and returned home.

The Israelis wanted Arafat to relinquish his people's claims to East Jerusalem, give Israel much of the West Bank territory, and forgo the U.N.-sanctioned Palestinian right to return to homes that are now part of the nation of Israel. Arafat was unwilling to do this. He is a man who is thinking of his people, his nation, and his own place in history, at all times. To give up so much to the Israelis would mean losing face, and Arafat is not about to lose face willingly . . . ever.

His thinking during the Camp David meeting must also surely have been influenced by the success of the Hezbollah military group's success in pushing the Israelis out of Lebanon completely. Just prior to the meetings at Camp David, the Israelis withdrew unconditionally from South Lebanon. Arafat wanted what the Lebanese had received, but Israel's Prime Minister Barak was unwilling to give it to him.

In late September of 2000, the Israeli right-wing opposition leader, Ariel Sharon, visited a Jerusalem site known as the Temple Mount to Jews and as Haram al-Sharif, or Nobel Sanctuary, to Muslims. His visit sparked the anger of crowds of Palestinians in Gaza and the West Bank.

Angry Palestinians soon began attacking Israeli security forces. Violence escalated on both sides. Disgruntled by the continued violence, Israelis began to withdraw support for Prime Minister Barak. Explosions in Jerusalem and the northern Israeli port city of Haifa, which killed at least twenty-five Israelis and three suicide bombers during the month of December, led to renewed Israeli military strikes against Palestinian targets in the West Bank and Gaza. A second, much more violent Intifada broke out in Palestine.

In response to public criticism, Barak resigned in December of 2000. A special prime minister election was held in February of 2001, and Ariel Sharon was elected Prime Minister of Israel on February 6, 2001. Arafat and Sharon have a long history of enmity between them, so this did not bode well for the peace process.

Once again, the tit-for-tat violence between Israel and the Palestinians was devastating the Middle East. The hatred between Sharon and Arafat only added wood to the fire. The international community condemned the continued killing

Claiming to be protecting themselves against terrorists, the Israelis invaded the West Bank in 2002, killing civilians and isolating Arafat in his PLO headquarters. Immediately, the Palestinian community held protests against Israel.

of Palestinians by the Israelis, but Sharon was unrepentant.

In early January of 2002, a three-week decrease in violence was ended when the Islamic militant group Hamas took credit for the death of four Israeli soldiers.

On January 18, 2002, tanks rolled into Ramallah and surrounded Arafat's headquarters. The military operation was instituted in response to an attack on a Bat Mitzvah for a young Israeli girl in northern Israel that left six people dead. Israeli Prime Minister Sharon, angered by ongoing suicide bombings staged by Palestinians against Israeli civilians, declared that Arafat was basically a prisoner of Israel.

Demonstrations broke out on the Gaza Strip in protest of the Israeli imprisonment of Arafat within his Ramallah compound. Over ten thousand protesters took to the streets calling for Arafat's release. Once again, in acting out against

Arafat, the Israelis had seemingly helped his cause, renewing his importance in the eyes of the Palestinian people and the Arab community at large.

By February of 2002, Arafat had, seemingly, grown quite comfortable under siege. Indeed, he seemed to be basking in the spotlight of the international media. The Israelis were occupying his compound, imprisoning him, just as they occupied the lands of his people and imprisoned his people. Playing the role of persecuted freedom fighter was second nature to Arafat by now. The Israelis set the stage for him, and he defiantly responded by beginning a series of monologues and dialogues publicized by the media.

His situation, and the decrease of Palestinian actions against civilians, began to garner worldwide support for Arafat and against Sharon. Arafat's forces and Palestinian militant groups focused their efforts on attacks on Israeli military targets and settlers of occupied territory. This allowed Arafat to argue that the strikes were legitimate acts of resistance, as opposed to acts of terrorism.

The United States publicly called for Prime Minister Sharon to refrain from doing any harm to Arafat. The international community called for the Israeli withdrawal from Palestine, but Sharon refused. When urged to allow Arafat to attend an upcoming Arab summit, Sharon demanded that Arafat put an end to all terrorist strikes against Israel.

Under the advisement of the United States government, Sharon relented and stated publicly that Arafat would be allowed to attend the Arab summit, if he so desired. Sharon would not, however, guarantee that Arafat would be allowed to return to his compound in Ramallah. On March 27, 2002, the key Arab summit took place without Arafat in attendance.

Arafat announced that he would not desert his people in their time of need to attend the Arab summit in Beirut. Instead, he told them that he was standing with them, resilient and ever defiant in the face of continued and escalating Israeli

Suicide bombings became sadly commonplace in Israel in 2002. Israelis were outraged by a bombing in March in which a Palestinian attacked a crowd celebrating Passover in a hotel dining room.

aggression. He also was resolved against providing the Israeli government with a chance to prevent him from returning to Ramallah and to his people.

The same day that Arafat was to attend the Arab summit in Beirut, a rash of suicide bombings began.

In the Israeli resort of Netanya, a Palestinian suicide bomber blew himself up at a hotel. The bomber died, killing twenty-two Israelis who were celebrating Passover at the time. Two days later, on March 29, 2002, a Palestinian woman blew herself up at a Jewish supermarket, killing two other people. On March 30, a suicide attack was staged on a Tel Aviv restaurant. The bomber died and Israelis were wounded.

On that same day, the U.N. held an emergency assembly to address the situation in Palestine. Norway sponsored a solution to the situation at hand under the name of U.N. Resolution 1402. The plan called for the withdrawal of Israeli troops from

Palestinian cities, including Ramallah, for action on the parts of Israel and Palestine toward a cease fire, cooperation of both parties with U.S. Envoy Anthony Zinni, and for an end to "all acts of terror, provocation, incitement, and destruction."

On March 31, Palestinian violence against Israelis exploded once more. Another suicide bomber attacked a restaurant in Haifa in northern Israel. The bomber killed himself, as well as fourteen Israeli Jews and Arabs. On the very same day, another bomber killed himself and wounded four people in an attack on a paramedics office in the Jewish settlement of Efrat, south of Bethlehem.

In response to the bombings, United States President George W. Bush urged Arafat to put an end to the violence. "He's got to make it absolutely clear that the Palestinian Authority does not support these terrorist activities," Bush told the press. He pleaded with Arafat to seek peace and to condemn terrorism.

Forty to forty-five foreign activists joined Arafat in a show of support for the Palestinian leader and his cause on March 31, 2002. The image of a smiling Arafat was broadcast on major television networks throughout the world, as he met with them in his compound. Nine of the activists tried to leave later in the evening, but they were arrested by Israeli forces outside the compound. Many of the activists chose to remain in the compound with Arafat and promised to act as human shields to protect him from the Israelis, if need be.

On April 2, 2002, Israeli tanks continued into Bethlehem. Along the West Bank, Israeli troops searched for militants. The Palestinian security headquarters near Ramallah was invaded by Israeli troops, as well.

Arafat was now being held in a closed military zone. The Israelis were no longer allowing media access to Arafat and his compound. In fact, they had expelled an American team of journalists from Ramallah to avoid allowing Arafat any chance to obtain further air time.

International journalists denounced Israeli forces for their interference with the press. In attempting to keep the press from contacting Arafat, Israel once again had pushed his name to the front pages of history. The international press cried out angrily for access to Arafat and the city of Ramallah.

Prime Minister Sharon and Foreign Minister Peres of Israel voiced different opinions on what should be done with Arafat. Sharon made statements offering to allow foreign diplomats to remove Arafat from Ramallah on the condition he never return to the area. Peres, on the other hand, issued statements opposing the use of force against Arafat.

The British Broadcasting Corporation (BBC) reported on April 2, 2002, that Arafat's Senior Palestinian Negotiator, Saeb Erekat, had stated that Arafat would "under no circumstances" accept exile. Erekat continued on to say that he feared that Arafat would be assassinated if this happened. Neither the tactic of assassination or exile of Arafat by Israel is supported by the United States.

Assassinating Arafat might end his rule of the Palestinian people, but it would not end his influence over them. In fact, assassination would only serve to further immortalize Arafat in the eyes of his people. Exiling the leader, according to U.S. Secretary of State Colin Powell, would only allow Arafat to "conduct the same kinds of activities and give the same messages that he is giving now." Additionally, the assassination or exile of Arafat might serve to completely enrage the Arab and Palestinian communities, leading the Middle East into another major war.

Meanwhile, Israel and Palestine are at war. Gun battles between Israeli soldiers and Palestinian militia have exploded in Bethlehem and Ramallah. The Israeli forces have reoccupied towns along the West Bank. Prime Minister Sharon is intent on destroying what he and the Israelis see as the Palestinian terrorist infrastructure. According to Sharon, Arafat will not do this, so the Israelis must.

Arafat waits out the Israeli invasion in his Ramallah compound, where he has been surrounded by Israeli tanks, in this April 1, 2002, photo. On April 28, 2002, the United States helped negotiate a deal between Israel and the Palestinians that allowed Arafat to go free.

Arafat will not accept exile from his homeland. Erakat indicated this by stating quite simply: "I don't think anyone in a sane mind would accept exile from his own country." Therefore, Arafat sits and waits in a compound surrounded by Israelis. The aging leader may be running short of supplies and medication, but his dreams of a Palestinian nation with him as its leader are replenished nightly.

He is only visibly armed with a cell phone and a submachine gun. Still, Arafat has the Palestinian people on his side. He has a roomful of foreign activists willing to act as human body armor for him. Their presence tells Arafat that the world at large sees him and understands his people's desire to establish a nation free from the oppression of the Zionists. The U.N. has asked Israel to withdraw, and Arafat sees this as a sign of support, as well.

On April 28, 2002, Arafat once again proved himself to be seemingly indestructible when the Israelis and Palestinians reached an agreement, with the intervention of the United States, to allow Arafat to leave his compound and travel freely in Palestinian territory. To arrange the deal, however, Arafat had to agree to allow the imprisonment of six Palestinians wanted by the Israelis for terrorist activities. Despite this concession, the deal is a small victory for Arafat.

Now well over seventy years old, Arafat is still Mr. Palestine in his own mind and in the minds of his people. His determination to remain forever the symbol of Palestine is best summarized in his own words: "They want me under arrest or in exile or dead, but I am telling them, I prefer to be martyred." And Arafat will remain the symbol of Palestine: a terrorist to some, a freedom fighter to others.

1929 Born in Cairo, Egypt, August 4 or 24.

1947 Arafat establishes ties to the Grand Mufti of Jerusalem.

1948 Arafat settles in Cairo, where he studies engineering at University of Cairo.

1952 He joins the Muslim Brotherhood and Union of Palestinian Students.

1956 Arafat fights in the Suez Campaign for the Egyptian Army.

1956 Moves to Kuwait, works as an engineer, and establishes his own company.

1957 Starts al-Fatah. Al-Fatah conducts several attacks in Israel.

1967 Al-Fatah becomes connected to PLO.

1968 Arafat elected chairman of PLO.

1974 Arafat addresses the United Nations General Assembly.

1982 The PLO moves from Lebanon after Israel invasion. Arafat sets up headquarters in Tunisia.

1988 State of Palestine proclaimed at a meeting on November 15 in Algiers, Algeria.

1989 Arafat elected president of State of Palestine by the Central Council of the Palestine National Council.

1991 United States-led talks begin in Madrid, Spain, but lead nowhere.

1993 Oslo agreement pursues a "land for peace" principle. Arafat recognizes Israel's right to exist.

1994 Israeli forces withdraw from Jericho in May. Arafat returns to Palestine in July.

1995 Arafat wins the Nobel Prize for Peace.

1996 Elected president of the Palestinian Authority in public elections on January 20, Arafat receives an overwhelming 88% of the votes.

1999 Memorandum signed by Arafat and Ehud Barak at Sharm el-Sheikh redefines the timeline for application of the Wye River Memorandum on further redeployment of the Israeli army.

1999 Likud leader Ariel Sharon's visit to the al-Aqsa precinct in Jerusalem, Islam's third holiest place, triggers Palestinian demonstrations. President Arafat describes the visit as a dangerous affront to Islam's holy places.

1999 Extraordinary 25th Arab summit in Cairo. The participants accuse Israel of conducting "a war against the Palestinian people."

1999 In November, Arafat and Peres meet for peace talks.

1999 A December summit at Sharm al-Sheikh between Barak, Arafat, U.S. President Bill Clinton, and Egyptian President Hosni Mubarak is cancelled.

1999 Israel rejects Palestinian sovereignty over the Aqsa compound in Jerusalem; the Palestinians refuse to give up the principle of the refugees' right of return.

2001 Israeli-Palestinian negotiations restart in Washington. Clinton fails to broker a lasting peace for the Middle East.

2002 Intifada breaks out in September.

2002 Arafat placed under house arrest.

2002 In late March, Israeli troops begin campaign to oust terrorists from Palestine. Arafat remains under house arrest and is cut off from the media.

2002 On March 30 the U.N. calls for the withdrawal of Israeli troops from Palestinian cities, including Ramallah, for action on the parts of Israel and Palestine toward a cease-fire, cooperation of both parties with U.S. Envoy Anthony Zinni, and for an end to "all acts of terror, provocation, incitement, and destruction."

2002 Early in April, Israeli troops continue to move forward into Palestine. There is no withdrawal of troops in sight. Sharon offers Arafat the chance to leave and remain in exile. A spokesman for Arafat vehemently refuses such a plan.

Carter, Jimmy. *Blood of Abraham.* Houghton Mifflin, 1985.

Chacour, Elias. *Blood Brothers.* Chosen/Zondervan, 1984.

Finkelstein, Norman G. *Image and Reality of the Israel-Palestine Conflict.* Verso, 1995.

Flapan, Simha. *The Birth of Israel: Myths and Realities.* Pantheon, 1987.

———. *Zionism and the Palestinians.* Barnes & Noble, 1979.

Gerner, Deborah J. *One Land, Two Peoples: The Conflict over Palestine.* 2d ed. Westview, 1994. (3d ed. expected in January of 2003.)

Hart, Alan. *Arafat.* Indiana University Press, 1984.

Hertzberg, Arthur. *The Zionist Idea.* Atheneum, 1959.

Hirst, David. *The Gun and the Olive Branch: The Roots of Violence in the Middle East.* Faber & Faber, 1984.

Khouri, Fred J. *The Arab-Israeli Dilemma.* Syracuse University Press, 1968.

Laqueur, Walter, and Barry Rubin, eds. *The Israel-Arab Reader.* Penguin, 1984.

Lustick, Ian. *Arabs in a Jewish State.* University of Texas, 1980.

Masalha, Nur. *Imperial Israel and the Palestinians: The Politics of Expansion.* Pluto, 2000.

Morris, Benny. *1948 and After: Israel and the Palestinians.* Clarendon, 1994.

———. *The Origin of the Palestinian Refugee Problem, 1947–49.* Cambridge University Press, 1988.

———. *Righteous Victims: A History of the Zionist-Arab Conflict, 1881–1999.* Knopf, 1999.

Oz, Amos. *In the Land of Israel.* Harcourt Brace Jovanovich, 1983.

Rubenstein, Danny. *The Mystery of Arafat.* Steerforth Press, 1995.

Sabini, John. *Islam: A Primer.* Middle East Editorial Associates, 1717 Massachusetts Ave. NW, Washington, D.C.

Said, Edward. *The Question of Palestine.* Vintage, 1980.

Shlaim, Avi. *The Iron Wall: Israel and the Arab World.* W.W. Norton, 2001.

Smith, Charles. *Palestine and the Arab-Israeli Conflict.* St. Martin's Press, 1992.

Abu Hassan, 59
Abu Iyad (Salah Khalaf), 37, 46, 54, 57-58, 59
Abu Jihad (Khalil al-Wazir), 37, 39, 42, 46, 57, 58, 59
Abu Lutf (Farouk Kaddoumi), 37
Abu Said (Khaled al-Hassan), 37
Adwan, Kamal, 59
Airline hijacking campaign, 52-53
Al-Fatah, 37-39, 41, 42
    and Arafat as spokesman, 47
    and battle of Karameh, 47
    and Jordan, 55-56, 57-58
    and PLO, 42-44, 47
    and Six-Day War, 44-46
Algeria, and al-Fatah, 39
Al-Hassan, Khalid, 59
Amman Agreement, 55, 57
Arab-Israeli war (1948), 26, 28-31, 33, 71, 74
Arab League, 28, 41-42, 54
Arab summit
    1974, 62, 77
    2002, 96
Arafat, Suha Tawil (wife), 87-89, 91
Arafat, Yasir
    and Arab-Israli war (1948), 28-31
    and arms trade, 28
    and arrests, 35, 43, 44
    assassination or exile of, 99, 100
    birth of, 21-22
    childhood of, 22-25, 31
    daughter of, 91
    education of, 22, 23, 25, 26, 28, 33
    and Egyptian army, 37
    as engineer, 26, 33, 37, 41
    family of, 22-26
    and full name, 21
    and Iraqi invasion of Kuwait, 89
    and Islam, 25
    and marriage, 87-89, 91
    and Mufti of Palestine, 26, 28
    and Nasser, 35-37, 55
    and Palestinian cause, 14-18, 28-31, 33-34, 37-38, 43, 49, 58, 65-81

See also Al-Fatah; Palestinian Liberation Organization
    and peace efforts, 18-19, 60-63, 65-81, 87, 89-90, 93-94
    as president of Palestinian Authority, 90
    as prisoner of Israel, 95-101
    and Suez Canal battles, 34-35
    as symbol of Palestine, 14-19, 31, 58, 61, 63, 101
    and Syria, 38-39
    and terrorism, 59-60, 62, 69-79, 87, 98
    and U.N., 62-63, 65-81, 83, 101
    uniform of, 14, 49, 65
    and "Yasir" as nickname, 25
    and Yom al-Nakba (2001), 14-19
Arafat, Zahwa (daughter), 91
Assad, Hafez, 62

Barak, Ehud, 94
Bedouins, 28, 52, 56
Begin, Menachem, 28
Ben Bella, Amhad, 39
Ben-Gurion, David, 30
Bethlehem, 98, 99
Black September Organization (BSO), 59
Bush, George W., 98

Cairo Agreement, 54-55, 57
Camp David meeting, 93-94

Deir Yassin, 28

Egypt
    and al-Fatah, 41, 43, 44
    Arafat's early years in, 22, 23-26, 28-29, 33-34
    and Gaza Strip, 33, 35, 44
    and Golan Heights, 62
    and Great Britain, 34-35
    and Nasser, 35-37, 41, 43, 44, 55
    and Palestine, 28, 30, 35-36
    and Sadat, 55, 62
    and Six-Day War, 44

and Suez Canal battles, 34-35
   and Syria, 38
Egyptian-Jordanian initiative, 19
Egyptian Union of Students, 33-34
Erekat, Saeb, 99, 100

Farouk, King of Egypt, 35
Fedayeen (self-sacrificers), 35-36
Filastinuna (Our Palestine), 37

Gaza Strip, 33, 35, 44, 87, 89, 94, 95
Gemayel, Bashir, 86
General Union of Palestinian
   Students, 34
Geneva Conventions, 73
Golan Heights, 62, 72
Great Britain, 21, 34-35

Habash, George, 52, 59, 62
Hamas, 14, 95
Hezbollah, 94
Holy Strugglers, 28
Hussein, King of Jordan, 51, 52, 53,
   54, 55, 57-58
Hussein, Saddam, 89
Husseini, Abdel Kader al-, 28, 29
Husseini, Hajj Amin al-, 26

International legitimacy, 16, 19
Intifada
   1987, 87, 89
   2000, 94
Iraq, 39, 89
Irgun, 28
Israel, creation of, 13-14, 30
Israeli-Palestinian conflict
   in 2002, 95-96
   and al-Fatah, 43, 44, 47
   and Arab-Israeli war (1948), 26,
      28-31, 33, 71, 74
   and attack on Arafat's Tunisian
      headquarters, 86-87
   and Black September, 59-60
   and Gaza Strip, 35-36
   and Golan Heights, 62

and Lebanon, 83-86, 94
   and 1987 Intifada, 87, 89
   and PLO, 51-52, 54, 58, 59-60
   and Six-Day War, 44
   and 2000 Intifada, 94
   in 2002, 95-101
   and Yom al-Nakba (2001), 13-19

Jarring Peace Talks, 53
Jericho, 89
Jerusalem, 72, 74, 81, 93, 94
   Arafat's early years in, 22, 23
   and Palestine, 18
   and Six-Day War, 44, 46
Jordan
   and al-Fatah, 47
   and Black September, 59
   and PLO, 51-58
   and Six-Day War, 44
   and West Bank, 33, 44

Kahane Commission, 86
Karameh, battle of, 47
King Fuad I University (Cairo
   University), 26, 28-29, 33-34
Kissinger, Henry, 62, 65
Kuwait, Iraqi invasion of, 89

Lebanon
   and Israel, 84-86, 94
   and PLO, 57, 83-86
   and war between Muslims and
      Christians, 84, 86

Mitchell Committee, 19
Munich Olympics, 59-60
Muslim Brotherhood, 30, 34-35, 38, 44

Nablus, 46, 88
Naguib, Mohammed, 35
Nasser, Gamal Abdel, 35-37, 41, 43, 44
   and al-Fatah, 42
   and Arafat, 35-37, 55
   and PLO, 42
Nobel Peace Prize, 90

Oslo Accords, 89
Ottoman Empire, 21

Palestine, 74
  and Arafat, 14-18, 28-31, 33-34, 37-38, 43, 49, 58, 65-81. *See also* Al-Fatah; Palestinian Liberation Movement
  Arafat as symbol of, 14-19, 31, 58, 61, 63, 101
  and Egypt, 35-36
  and Great Britain, 21
  Mufti of, 26, 28
  partition of, 26, 28
  and refugees, 16, 18, 28, 33, 39, 46, 47, 58, 72, 74
  and U.N., 65
  and World War II armaments, 28
  See also Israeli-Palestinian conflict
Palestine National Council, 52, 87
Palestinian Authority, 89, 90, 98
Palestinian Council, 90
Palestinian Liberation Army (PLA), 54
Palestinian Liberation Organization (PLO), 41-44, 47, 62, 75-77
  and al-Fatah, 42-44, 47
  and Arab summit (1974), 62, 77
  and Arafat as chairman, 48-49
  and Black September, 59-60
  and Iraqi invasion of Kuwait, 89
  and Israel, 83-86
  and Jordan, 51-58
  and Lebanon, 83-86
  legitimacy of, 77
  and terrorism, 69-71
  and Tunisia, 86-87
  and U.N., 65
  and United States, 87
Palestinian Students' Association, 34
Peace process, 18-19
  and Arafat, 18-19, 60-63, 65-81, 83, 87, 89-90, 93-94
  and Egyptian-Jordanian initiative, 19
  and Mitchell Committee, 19
  and Oslo Accords, 89
  and U.N., 19, 97-98
Peres, Shimon, 99
Phalangists, 84
Popular Front for the Liberation of Palestine (PFLP), 52, 53, 54, 62
Powell, Colin, 99

Qaddoumi, Farouk, 54

Rabin, Yitzhak, 89
Ramallah, 46, 88, 95-101
Rejectionist Front, 62
Resolutions, of U.N., 16, 19, 97-98
Rifai, Abd al-Munim ar-, 52

Sadat, Anwar, 55, 62
Saoud, Sheikh Hassan Abul, 26, 28
Sharon, Ariel, 86, 94-95, 96, 99
Shukeiri, Ahmad, 42, 43-44
Sinai, 72
Sitta, Hamid Abu, 29
Six-Day War (1967), 44-46
Stern Gang, 28
Suez Canal battles, 34-35
Syria
  and al-Fatah, 44
  and Arafat, 38-39
  and Egypt, 38
  and Golan Heights, 62
  and Lebanon, 84, 85
  and Palestine, 28
  and PLO, 54
  and Six-Day War, 44

Tapline pipe, 44
Tel, Wasif, 59
Temple Mount/Haram al-Sharif, 94
Thunderstorm (al-Assifa), 44
Transjordanian Arab Legion, 31
Tunisia, and PLO, 86-87

United Arab Republic, 38
United Nations
  and Arafat, 62-63, 65-81, 83, 101

and Israeli invasion of Lebanon, 84, 86
and Palestine, 65
and partition of Palestine, 26
and peace efforts, 19, 97-98
and PLO, 65, 86
Resolutions of, 16, 19, 97-98
United States
  and Arafat, 62-63, 65, 83, 87, 96, 98, 99, 101
  and Israeli invasion of Lebanon, 85-86
  and Sharon, 96

Voice of Palestine, The, 34

West Bank, 33, 44, 46, 87, 89, 93, 94, 98, 99

Yassin, Ahmad, 14
Yom al-Nakba (Day of Catastrophe, 2001), 13-19
Young Egypt, 34

Zinni, Anthony, 98
Zionism, 68-69, 71-74, 76-77, 79, 101

PICTURE CREDITS

2:    AP/Wide World Photos
11:   21st Century Publishing
12:   AFP/NMI
15:   AFP/NMI
17:   AP/Wide World Photos
19:   AP/Wide World Photos
20:   New Millennium Images
24:   AP/Wide World Photos
27:   Austrian Archives/Corbis
29:   AP/Wide World Photos
30:   AP/Wide World Photos
32:   New Millennium Images
36:   AP/Wide World Photos
40:   Hulton/Archive by Getty Images
45   AP/Wide World Photos
48:   AP/Wide World Photos
50:   AP/Wide World Photos

53:   Hulton/Archive by Getty Images
56:   Hulton/Archive by Getty Images
61:   Bettmann/Corbis
63:   Hulton/Archive by Getty Images
64:   AP/Wide World Photos
70:   Hulton/Archive by Getty Images
73:   Bettmann/Corbis
76:   Francoise de Mulder/Corbis
80:   AP/Wide World Photos
82:   AP/Wide World Photos
85:   AP/Wide World Photos
88:   AP/Wide World Photos
90:   AFP/NMI
92:   AP/Wide World Photos
95:   AP/Wide World Photos
97:   AP/Wide World Photos
100: AP/Wide World Photos

Cover: AP/Wide World Photos

ABOUT THE AUTHOR

COLLEEN MADONNA FLOOD WILLIAMS is the wife of Paul Williams and the mother of Dillon Meehan. She holds a bachelor's degree in elementary education with a minor in art. Colleen is the author of over ten nonfiction books for children and young adults.

ARTHUR M. SCHLESINGER, jr. is the leading American historian of our time. He won the Pulitzer Prize for his book *The Age of Jackson* (1945) and again for a chronicle of the Kennedy Administration, *A Thousand Days* (1965), which also won the National Book Award. Professor Schlesinger is the Albert Schweitzer Professor of the Humanities at the City University of New York and has been involved in several other Chelsea House projects, including the series REVOLUTIONARY WAR LEADERS, COLONIAL LEADERS, and YOUR GOVERNMENT.